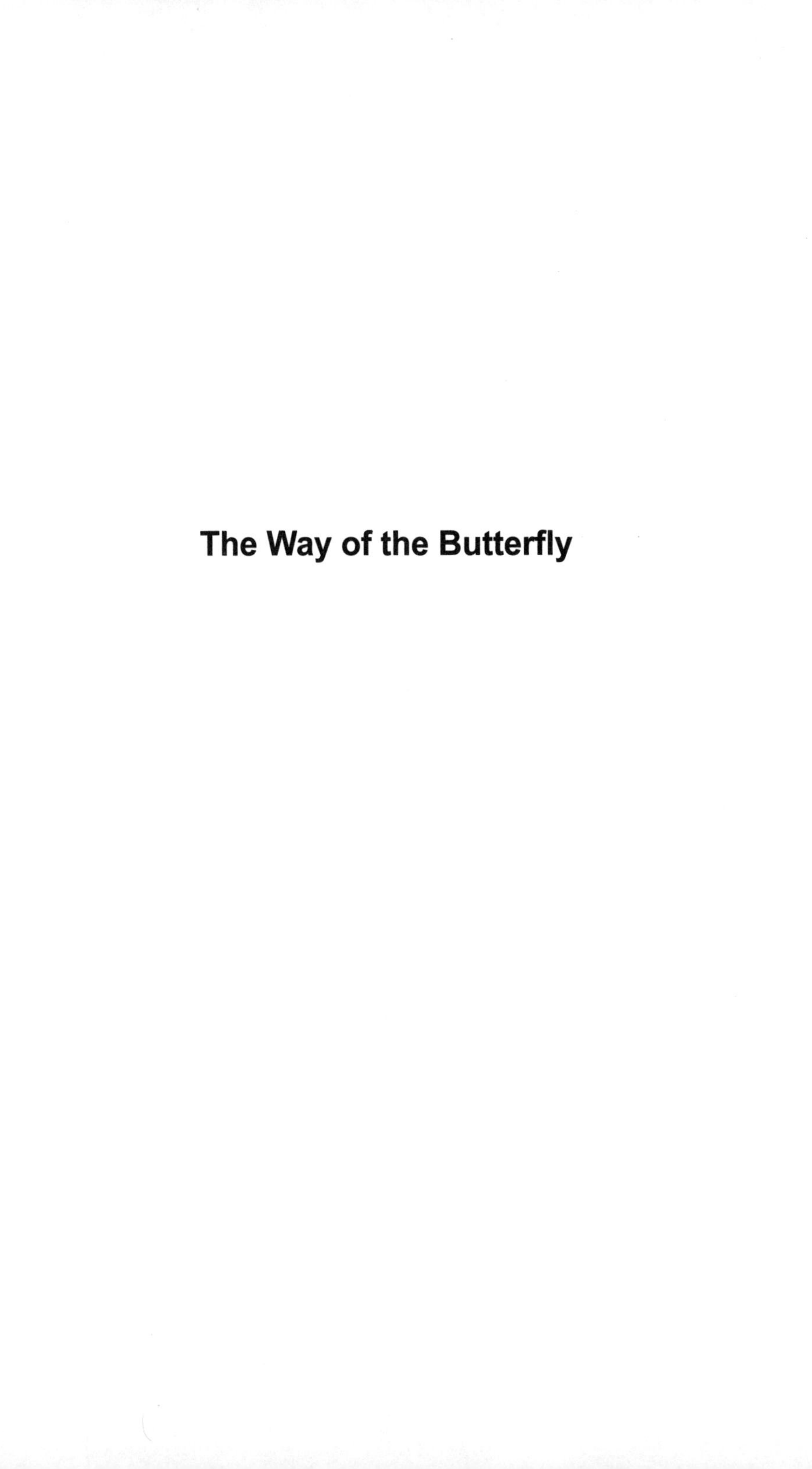

The Way of the Butterfly

The Way of the Butterfly

A Scientific Speculation on God and the Hereafter

JIM RIGAS

Author of
Christianity without Fairy Tales:
When Science and Religion Merge

ISBN=10 0-9794969-0-X (hard cover)
0-9794969-1-8 (soft cover)

Library of Congress Control Number: 2007932408

Published by Pnevma Publications, Chicago, IL.
Distributed by Pathway Book Service, Gilsum, NH.
(800) 345-6665 www.jimrigas.com

Printed by Professional Press
Chapel Hill, NC 27515-4371

Manufactured in the United States of America
07 08 09 10 11 7 6 5 4 3 2 1

To the memory of Judy

HÅGAR THE HORRIBLE

PREFACE

It is a rare person indeed who has gone through life without ever wondering what it's all about. But it seems that most of the time we are too busy working or playing to worry about such matters. We are always either cramming for tests at school, staying up late to finish a project for work, or rushing in three directions at once trying to neaten up and feed, wash, and tuck the kids into bed at night. Even when we are playing we still remain too busy to think. But occasionally one finds some quiet time, alone or with friends, to wonder why the hamster keeps racing on his wheel all day long despite the fact that he isn't getting anywhere. In general, however, it is only after a person retires that he has time to pursue such matters.

Perhaps the most depressing reading in literature can be found in the middle of the Bible, in the Book of Ecclesiastes. Looking back at his life, old man Qoheleth pronounces that everything in the world is just vanity: wisdom, riches, fame, toil, pleasure, all are passing. In the end "the dust returns to the earth as it was once, and the life-giving breath returns to God who gave it" (Ecc. 12:7). We usually tend to concentrate on the first half of this sentence. "Remember that you are dust and to dust you shall return," says the priest as he marks a cross on the forehead of the faithful on Ash Wednesday. But what about the second half of the sentence? What about the part that returns to God? That is the subject of this book.

Like most people my age, I spent my entire life studying, working, and raising a family. Although I took the kids to church, I never had much time to worry about what it all meant. But eventually I retired and I finally had some free time to think back on my life and try to make sense of some unusual incidents that occurred along the way. These had caused me to wonder not about the purpose of life but about what comes afterwards. Being a scientist, I did what scientists do. I did some research, read some books, thought about the matter. Scientists also perform experiments, and although an experiment would have given an unquestionable true and final answer, I held back. In some cases even a scientist has to remain satisfied with theory and forego actual tests.

I eventually published the results of my inquiry in my first book, *Christianity without Fairy Tales: When Science and Religion Merge.* In almost five hundred pages of what I believe to be a scholarly but highly readable study, I reviewed the historical unfolding of the Judeo-Christian religion from the story of Creation to the development of the Nicene Creed, and compared it to related scientific breakthroughs: archaeological discoveries in the Middle East, linguistic analyses of the Bible, the evolution theories of Charles Darwin and Alfred Wallace, the Big Bang theory, as well as the more avant-garde cosmological hypotheses of David Bohm and Rupert Sheldrake. It was meant to be a scientific endeavor, however, laying out the groundwork but not answering specific questions; such answers are personal opinions and I had always intended to present them in a separate book—this one.

I do not plan to revisit the previous discussion here, but I did conclude that although Scripture might be inspired it is not historically accurate. As a result I will not be presenting here any arguments that depend on the Bible for support, although I will occasionally refer to it. In contrast to my earlier book, this one is biographically anecdotal and discusses how my personal experiences have shaped my personal beliefs. I hope that the reader will accept the truth of my experiences even if he disagrees with my conclusions.

A word about the comic strips sprinkled throughout the book. As I got older I became aware that comic strips are particularly enjoyed by the very young and the relatively old. The young find something in the newspaper that they think they can understand, and the older readers, sick of all the bad news printed every day, are looking for something more pleasant. But many people also recognize that most cartoons do present insights into aspects of real life. I have also discovered that comics often reveal many interesting tidbits about current lifestyle and politics, as well as about the matters that I discuss in this book. Many times a cartoonist appears to have instinctively grasped the truth about a concept that I have struggled to understand, and has presented it in a crisp, concise manner. The cartoon about Sheldrake's Morphic Resonance Theory, for instance, smoothly relates a complex theoretical issue that I would have been afraid to bore the reader with. It is science cloaked as entertainment. Many other comic strips are included just to lighten up an otherwise heavy subject. Do let me know which one is your favorite. I would like to thank here all the artists and their agents who have so graciously allowed me to reproduce these cartoons in this book. Individual acknowledgments are presented in the captions and also in the List of Illustrations.

I would also like to thank Mrs. Barbara D. Hogan and Mr. Edward E. Tate, who read and suggested changes to the manuscript. Edward, a fellow engineer and the best man at my wedding a long time ago (he believes that the last qualifier should have been edited out as superfluous), is not a great admirer of my theological positions but was quick to question my scientific arguments and careless exaggerations. In contrast, I have never met Barbara in person, only on the Internet. But she is the only person I know who has read my first book three times. She was also kind enough to read this manuscript and honestly point out that the clarity of my original explanations of synchronicity and of David Bohm's theories resembled that of the Mississippi River during the spring flood season. It is not her fault if the sparkle of bottled Perrier has still eluded me. Finally I would like to thank my oldest daughter Maia, a professional editor, who took time from her busy schedule to read the manuscript and correct my idiosyncratic writing. Even more importantly, I have to thank her for showing me how to revamp much of my original writing so as to render the subject matter more interesting and reader-friendly. Since I personally made many last-minute corrections, however, she is not responsible for any errors that may have slipped in.

I have consciously tried to keep this book short. Hopefully, people who buy it will read it without delay, not save it for a long airplane flight to Australia—be warned, you will be finished before Hawaii.

CONTENTS

ILLUSTRATIONS AND ACKNOWLEDGMENTS

FOR BETTER OR WORSE

INTRODUCTION

High up in the courts of heaven today
  A little dog angel waits;
With the other angels he will not play,
  But he sits alone at the gates.
For I know my master will come, says he,
  And when he comes he will call for me.
The other angels pass him by
  As they hurry towards the throne,
And he watches them with a wistful eye
  As he sits at the gates alone.
But I know if I just wait patiently
  That someday my master will call for me.
And his master, down on earth below,
  As he sits in his easy chair,
Forgets sometimes, and whispers low
  To the dog, who is not there.
And the little dog angel cocks his ears,
  And dreams that his master's voice he hears.
And when at last his master waits
  Outside in the dark and cold,
For the hand of death to open the door,
  That leads to those courts of gold,
He will hear a sound through the gathering dark,
  A little dog angel's bark.

("A Little Dog-Angel" by Norah Holland, *Spun Yarn and Spindrift*.)

I have always felt drawn to this little poem, especially since Christian religion pronounces categorically that pets have no souls and that heaven, whatever it may be, has no room for them. But Christian religion could be wrong in this, as I'll contend in the following chapters.

Children first encounter death when a grandparent or pet dies: "He went to heaven and is with God now," is how we usually try to console them. But as children grow up and learn about science, they often put heaven in the same category as Santa Claus and the Tooth Fairy. Even the controversial Episcopal Bishop John Shelby Spong agreed with this when he asked, "Where is heaven?.... There appears to be no place in our universe for heaven" (*Why Christianity Must Change or Die,* pp. 10, 205). And without heaven, of course, there is no God, no soul, and no life after death. Another of my goals in the following chapters is to prove the good bishop wrong.

Scientists, too, disbelieve the existence of God, soul, and life after death, and I plan to prove them wrong also. Unfortunately, the word "prove" is a little too assertive. What I will actually do is carefully define my terms, present data, cite modern scientific hypotheses and theories, and finally draw conclusions indicating that our universe is not restricted to the materialistic aspects our senses experience; that there is much more to it than meets our eyes.

I am sorry to say, however, that I will not be able to categorically prove my position, either. The data I will be using do not permit laboratory duplication, and although the theories I will be quoting represent the very latest in scientific thought they are not accepted by all. This is why the book title includes the word "speculation" rather than "revolutionary discoveries," or some other equally extravagant term. Nevertheless, I believe that you are likely to find more truth about God, the soul, and the hereafter in the few pages of this book than in both your Bible and physics textbook combined.

We will start our search by examining the occurrence of little miracles. These are events that fulfill a need but have no discernible cause. But just like an expanding set of circular ripples in the pool indicates that something has probably happened at their center—perhaps a pebble was tossed in or a fish stuck its head out—a causeless event suggests that we don't have complete understanding of our environment. Unknown factors are present.

We will then consider the most commonly proposed cause of unexplainable events, God. I'll discuss first the Jewish God, then the Christian God, and finally I will define the attributes of the only God who is important to me: a God who cares for me and can affect me. Since it is this kind of God to whom we pray for things we want, we will look at prayers and their effectiveness. This, in turn, will reveal a God with unusual responses, one I will call, somewhat in jest, "the computer God."

We will next turn our attention to some unusual occurrences, which though widely reported remain unsubstantiated by science: ghosts, near-death experiences, and communications with the dead. Any of these, if true, would indicate the human ego's survival of physical death. Can these occurrences be real? If so, how do they affect our understanding of the world we live in?

We will then consider what kind of physical universe would be consistent with our findings so far and examine the avant-garde theories of David Bohm, Rupert Sheldrake, and other modern physicists. Instead of Newton's comfortable, solid material world, these theories posit a mathematical based energy universe of surrealistic dream-like substance. Having stripped away the restrictions of strictly Newtonian thinking we will now be free to think of a physical universe that allows human memories to survive physical death, a prerequisite for what I call a soul and for life after death. Inspiration, telepathy, reincarnation experiences, and prayer effectiveness are only a few of the problems readily explained in such a universe.

We will then return to the point from where we started, our normal everyday world, to examine the effect of the Judeo-Christian religion within human history; how its conflicting tenets of free will vs. predestination, judgment for committed sins vs. forgiveness through grace, affect our expectations of afterlife. Only after we throw away all preconceived ideas of divinely ordained punishments and rewards upon our death, will we be able to recognize humanity's future: the metamorphosis of the caterpillar to a chrysalis and the final release and freedom of the butterfly. We will then also be able to answer Hägar's question in the book's first cartoon: "What is the purpose of life?"

DILBERT

RING
RING
RING
EMERGENCY, YOU SAY?
CRISIS?
www.dilbert.com scottadams@aol.com

I'M LOSING MY FAITH IN COINCIDENCES.
5/29/03 © 2003 United Feature Syndicate, Inc.

CHAPTER 1

THERE IS MORE THAN MEETS THE EYE

Were you ever thinking of your friend Mary when suddenly, the phone rang and there she was, all primed up for a long conversation? Or were you ever idly whistling a tune while turning the radio on, only to hear the same song come out of the speaker? Disconcerting as such coincidences are, they are probably quite meaningless. How often, for instance, have you thought of Mary without her calling you? Or, for that matter, any of your other friends? Personally, I often think of our president and what he is doing in Washington, but if he has ever called me I was not in and he didn't leave a message.

All events that occur simultaneously, however, are not coincidences. When every instrument in the orchestra falls suddenly silent at the last measure of the symphony, it is not a coincidence. When that new girl you just met is planning to wash her hair on all the evenings you want to take her out, it is probably not a coincidence.

Nevertheless, some coincidences are more unusual than others. Sometimes, when we are emotionally supercharged by some event in our life, something little happens that is so strongly related to our emotional state that it acquires a disproportionately significant meaning. We call such a coincidence a "synchronicity." At other times a chance event happens that greatly affects our life: "If I had not paused to look at that display window, the falling glass would have killed me," is an example. We call such chance events miracles: "It was a miracle that I was not killed," is how we express our feeling. Although all synchronicities can be called miracles, the reverse is not true: synchronicities are related to our current emotional state, while miracles are events that unexpectedly fulfill our personal needs, known or unknown.

Neither miracles nor synchronicities can be explained by the accepted physical rules governing our universe, so our physicists insist that they don't exist; they label them instead "chance events." If they were honest they would have called them instead, "unexplainable events."

A Voice on the Radio

Yesterday...
All my troubles seemed so far away,
Now it looks as though they are here to stay,
Oh, I believe...in yesterday.

Suddenly...
I'm not half the man I used to be,
There's a shadow hanging over me,
Oh, yesterday...came suddenly...

Why she had to go I don't know.
She wouldn't say.
I said something wrong,
Now I long for yesterday.

Yesterday...
Love was such an easy game to play,
Now I need a place to hide away,
Oh, I believe...in yesterday...

("Yesterday," by John Lennon and Paul McCartney.)

Since I am not a Beatles aficionado, I had never heard this song, or at least remember having heard it, until one morning many years ago. It was two days after my wife's sudden death and I was driving to the grocery store with my two daughters to buy supplies for the luncheon that would follow the funeral, when the radio played it. The song's timeliness was so obvious that my eleven-year-old turned and looked at me intently. Acting like a macho man, however, I kept my eyes straight ahead on the road and pretended that I had not heard anything unusual. Thinking about it now, I wish that I had hugged her instead.

A year later I heard the song again. This time it was on the anniversary of my wife's death and I had sneaked out from work to buy a red rose to place on her grave. I was on my way to the cemetery, actually our church's Memorial Garden, when it came over the car radio again. So strange! Twenty more years passed before I heard it again, this time on a Carreras tape the kids gave me as a present.

At the time I considered these two events to be little miracles. I figured that somebody, somewhere, was trying to send me a message telling me that he empathized with me, that I was being thought of. After all, a miracle is just a fortuitous coincidence that fulfills a purpose. Many years later, however, I learned that these two occurrences could also be considered examples of what Carl G. Jung had called "synchronicities."

Synchronicity

Carl Jung was born in Switzerland in 1875. Originally he had wanted to become an archaeologist but, since that subject was not taught at the local university and his parents were poor, he settled for medicine, specializing in the new field of psychiatry. He became known for his work on the subconscious and postulated that it was somehow shared or inherited by all mankind. But he was also deeply interested in such occult subjects as alchemy, astrology, and Gnostic beliefs. According to Stephan Hoeller (*The Gnostic Jung*, p.18), "Jung's influence is almost solely responsible for the vital project of the publication of the greatest storehouse of original Gnostic writings ever discovered in history, the Nag Hammadi Library." The first translated portion from that library was even named after him, the Jung Codex.

Jung became intrigued by the observation that a person's emotional state was occasionally associated with highly unlikely external events that were very significant to that person in his emotional state. He defined synchronicity as the coincidental correspondence between a random event and the mental state of the observer who then attributes to this event semi-mystical importance.

Jung believed that the mental state does not give rise to the event but that in the universe they are somehow interconnected. He postulated that the human unconscious is part of the basic structure of the universe and that the two move in a tandem but acausal manner. He did not explain how this acausal relationship operated, but he did propose that the unconscious minds of all humans were connected, and he defined the result of this connectivity as God—not the Judeo-

Christian God, of course, but some kind of central power in the universe.

Interacting with the Universe

While the previous paragraph defines synchronicity, it does not explain it. We are asked, instead, to assume that the world apparently contains an infinite number of possibilities and that our intense emotional state at a particular time is somehow related to the actual possibility that materializes. It reminds me of the physics experiment where one hits a tuning fork inside a room full of tuning forks, causing those with the same natural frequency to also ring. In that experiment, however, there exists a direct cause-and-effect relationship between the first tuning fork that elicits the response, which we will call "us," and the ones reacting to it, which we will call "synchronicities."

This explanation implies that humans can directly affect their environment through their actions, thoughts, and emotions. If true, we are responsible not only for our own actions and thoughts but also for whatever else takes place in the world around us; we are in fact creating our own reality! Obviously, this paradigm differs somewhat from Jung's definition of synchronicity since the events it describes are directly cause-and-effect related.

The example of the tuning forks can be made to conform closer to Jung's postulate by introducing an adjustable-frequency sound generator in the room.

When it operates at the natural frequency of our tuning fork both our fork ("us") and those forks having the same natural frequency ("synchronicities") will resonate. This arrangement, however, removes all independence from the master fork, "us," as all ringing tuning forks are now reacting to an external source. We are describing here a world in which we are no longer masters of our fate but puppets responding to the strings of a hidden puppeteer. This scenario replaces the concept of free will with the idea of a controlling universe, one generated by something akin to David Bohm's implicate fields, which will be discussed in chapter 5.

But in addition to imposing total randomness or total control in the experiment, there is a third possibility. Suppose every tuning fork in the room has its own natural frequency. When our fork rings nothing happens. Occasionally, however, a giant hand reaches into the room and adjusts one fork's natural frequency setting it to that of our own fork so that they will now both vibrate in unison. This is a situation where neither are we pulling the strings of the world, nor is the world pulling ours. We are pretty much moving along our independent way in an independent world, except that we are occasionally being nudged along by an external and often unperceived gust of wind.

To summarize, the existence of synchronicities allows for three possible interpretations of the world in which we live:

(1) Our actions and emotions affect the reality of the universe around us. Not only do we write our own script in the play of life, but we can also manipulate to some extent those of others. (Our tuning fork activates other tuning forks.)

(2) Our actions and emotions are an inescapable result of the universe around us. We are all part of a grander whole that controls our actions and even our thoughts; much like a cork bobbing on top of the waves carried hither and yonder without any independent volition or apparent purpose. (The ringing of all tuning forks depends on the frequencies generated by the loudspeaker.)

(3) There exists an intelligent power, which we usually call God, that interferes in our lives, altering the reality around us. Although we believe that we write our own life scripts, in actuality this interested entity occasionally tweaks the randomness of our world around us to affect our lives. Somewhat like when in a football game an unexpected gust of wind helps our team kick a fifty-five-foot field goal. (An unknown external entity adjusts the natural frequency of a particular tuning fork in the room; my original thought when I heard that song on the radio.)

Of the three possibilities the second one is the most nihilistic. It would be the choice of Qoheleth, the author of the Book of Ecclesiastes whom we met in the preface: everything is preordained, so nothing matters. The other two possibilities offer us some hope of controlling our lives: in the first case directly through our own powers, even though we may be unaware of them; in the third by attempting to persuade a powerful external power to intercede on our behalf.

There is probably no way of differentiating between these two possibilities. Both cases involve wishing—praying, if you prefer. I can tell myself, “I can do it.” Or I can ask God, “Please do this for me.” Or I can combine both approaches and empower myself by saying, “Through God’s help I will be able do this.” But who is this God that will either do things for me or help me do them myself?

CANDORVILLE

CHAPTER 2

IS THERE A GOD?

By the term God, most people in the Western world usually mean the Judeo-Christian God described in the pages of the Bible. For the atheists, those who don't believe in God, it is this particular God that they don't believe in. They will argue that the Bible is wrong, that the God it portrays cannot exist, and that since he does not exist they will generalize to conclude that no God of any kind exists.

With the ascendancy of science and the rise of modern archaeology, many theologians have come to reject the existence of the Bible's omnipotent, omniscient, creator God and have been drawn to more abstract concepts of divinity. They will proclaim that God and the universe are one, or that God is love. Such deistic Gods, however, are not directly involved with human concerns—and as a practical engineer I find them irrelevant. For me, a God who will not help me when I ask for help is a useless God. I prefer to define a God with fewer attributes but one to whom I can pray and who can respond to me. I will present my definition of God at the end of the chapter, where I will list the minimum requirements that such a God needs to meet in order to be relevant. We will then spend the rest of the book looking for him or, more correctly, for it.

Yahweh, the Hebrew God

In Western society when somebody uses the word *God* he almost always means Yahweh, or Jehovah, the God of the Hebrews whom Christians call the Father. The Old Testament books describe him as a powerful deity, the most powerful deity, in fact, one who adopted the Hebrew people as the nation to serve him and then spent the next two thousand years alternately protecting and chastising them.

Yahweh is presented as a sometimes irascible God who often demanded the complete annihilation of his enemies; all those who lived in the lands he intended to deed to his favorite people or who worshiped other gods. Justice was his distinguishing characteristic. This was interpreted by the Hebrew people to mean that every misstep of his people, willful or accidental, had to be punished in proper measure. Most minor lapses, however, and events involving uncontrolled discharge of certain body fluids could be forgiven by performing various detailed rituals involving either full immersion in water or the sacrifice of innocent animal life.

Biblical writers attributed to Yahweh three additional characteristics: omnipotence, omniscience, and goodness. These claims, however, are not found in the Pentateuch (Genesis through Deuteronomy) or in the Historical Books of the Old Testament (Joshua through Nehemiah). Indeed, the God Yahweh is often portrayed in them as someone who himself makes mistakes that reveal a lack of foreknowledge and someone who has difficulty achieving his goals. Time after time his apparent solution to a problem is to almost annihilate his own creation, his own people. Moreover, ascribing to God these three attributes raises the question that has never been answered satisfactorily: if the God Yahweh is indeed omniscient, omnipotent, and good, why does he allow so much evil to exist in the world? We will address this question in chapter 9.

Our knowledge of Yahweh derives from the Old Testament, particularly its first seven books. Genesis contains some mythical descriptions of the creation of the earth and its inhabitants; of a talking snake that tricks the first humans into ignoring the command of God their Father (my children do it all the time without the intervention of a snake); and finally of a enormous flood that kills all living things in God's creation except for what could fit into a boat the size of a mini-aircraft-carrier built by a six-hundred-year-old man and his three sons. Exodus relates an epic story of a single devout man who, with God's help, leads two million people out of Egypt's enslavement into the desert. There they encounter God, put him inside a gold-plated box, and cart him with them through the desert for forty years until they finally reach Canaan, the land of the patriarchs. The books of Numbers, Deuteronomy, and Joshua describe how the Hebrew people conquer that land, kill most of its inhabitants, and settle in.

Except, of course, that all these stories are not history but legends, fables, or fairy tales: God did not create the world as described in Genesis, there was no talking snake in the Garden of Eden, everybody and everything in the world did not drown in a flood; six hundred thousand men of fighting age with their wives, children, and livestock, plus the tribe of Levites, did not wander through the desert for forty years and, even if any did, they did not emerge to conquer Canaan as described. As for putting God inside a box, I will leave this for you to decide.

Until the sixteenth century, it was taken for granted that Moses, the hero of the Exodus, was the author of the first five books of the Old Testament, with God himself dictating the book of Genesis. After all, this is what the Bible itself said. Then a few brave souls questioned that idea, pointing out that some kings named in the writings were born after Moses' death; but these people were either publicly disgraced or executed by the Church. A few more centuries had to pass before their ideas finally prevailed. Modern linguists and historians now tell us that six separate persons authored the Pentateuch and the Historical Books of the Old Testament, sometime between 800 BC and 430 BC, many years after the described events. Most archaeologists believe that neither the Exodus nor a military conquest of Canaan took place. Yet no one seems to question the God part of the stories.

The Father, Son, and Holy Spirit: The Christian God

In addition to Jews, Christians and Muslims also accept as true the Old Testament stories. The Muslims, however, add the Surahs from the Holy Qur'an, which contain the words of Prophet Mohammad. The Christians add the four canonical Gospels and numerous Letters, which make up the New Testament that deals with Jesus Christ, the Son of the Father.

In the New Testament God sends his one and only son to earth in the form of a human, named Jesus, to prepare mankind for the coming of God's Reign. He is crucified, resurrected, and ascends to heaven. Eventually his followers start a new religion, Christianity, and spend the first three centuries trying to figure out who exactly this Jesus was. At the famous Council of Nicaea they decide that he was God, one being with the Father and the Holy Spirit, all indivisible from each other but each one a separate entity—a definition that nobody has ever been able to explain successfully but that still remains the central doctrine of Christianity.

What is fascinating is that although the Old Testament Yahweh is the same entity as the New Testament Father, their personalities are poles apart. Yahweh is a creator, he makes things; the Father is a procreator, he procreates children. The difference between the two is like night and day. If you create paintings and you find them defective you can burn them and start new ones. But if you procreate children, even if you are unhappy with them, you have no choice but to accept them.

Most of modern Christianity is based on seven letters that Paul wrote between 48 AD and 62 AD. Paul was a Jew who had originally persecuted the early Christians but later experienced a miraculous conversion in which he saw a bright light and heard the voice of Jesus. He then became an ardent Christian and was the first to ascribe semi-divine characteristics to Jesus. Paul constructed an elaborate logical line of reasoning to conclude that Jesus had pre-existed creation and was the first-born of this creation; through his death and resurrection he conquered Satan gaining for humankind forgiveness for the original sin of the first human couple. Paul was the first to proclaim that if we believe in Jesus we will never die, and that if we do die we will be resurrected in a new spiritual body when Jesus returns to earth.

GET FUZZY

HOW DARE YOU STUPID CROCS TRY TO KILL ME IN MY OWN BED!! DIE!!! DIE!! DIE!!!
Whoa whoa Whoa whoa Whoa
Love you enemys.
SMACK
darb

I'M MORE OF AN OLD TESTAMENT GUY.

Of the four gospels that the Church recognizes as God-inspired, the first three describe the actions, teachings, death, and resurrection of a wise rabbi who, in Matthew's and Luke's gospels, was born through the immaculate conception of a virgin. This rabbi goes around preaching about his Father, who loves mankind and who wants to save it from final perdition. The fourth gospel, the Gospel according to John, expands on Paul's ideas and presents a Jesus who predates creation, who insists that he and the Father are one, and who is obsessed with the idea that the priestly establishment wants to kill him, something that eventually does come to pass. The main teaching of the Jesus portrayed in John's Gospel is that only those who believe in him will be saved; everyone else will fall into the hands of Satan.

The four gospels were probably written between 67 AD and 100 AD by unknown writers. The early belief that the gospels were written by some of Jesus' own disciples has been discarded except for the possibility that Luke, the author of the third gospel and of the Acts of the Apostles, may have actually traveled with Paul in the fifties.

The first followers of Jesus were Galilean and Jerusalem Jews who were personally acquainted with him. None of them thought he was God, although some did believe, perhaps, that he was the long-awaited Messiah. This Messiah, however, was singularly unsuccessful in fulfilling the goals widely expected of him, something that forced the new Christians to rewrite the Messiah's job description. Unfortunately, most of these Jewish Christians died when the Romans invaded Jerusalem in 70 AD, torching the city and killing almost all of its inhabitants. Most of the remaining Christians were the Gentile followers of Paul, the inventor of the mystical God-man Christ Jesus. This conception was strengthened in the later Gospel of John and provides the groundwork for Christianity.

The Christians of the second to fourth centuries AD, however, faced a logical impasse. In order to release mankind from the original sin of Adam and Eve, and in order for humanity to attain eternal life, Jesus had to be a God. But how could that be reconciled with both the basic Hebrew dogma that there exists only one God, and with the gospels that describe Jesus praying to his Father, another God? As we saw earlier this was accomplished, somewhat forcibly, at the Council of Nicaea, which gave birth to the basic Christian doctrine, the Nicene Creed, that is faithfully recited today in most churches but remains intellectually incomprehensible.

Searching for God

"God is beyond our comprehension," we are told by most of our religious leaders. But it is difficult to pray to something you do not comprehend. This is why people pray to Jesus, a man they can visualize who came, lived, and suffered among us, and to Mary, a mother with whom most women can empathize directly. That's why most pastors and denominations make an attempt to present some kind of a physical God-image to their congregations.

To Evangelical Christians God is just Jesus' father, and Jesus said that "Whoever has seen me has seen my Father." Then they quickly change the subject before people ask the obvious question. The literalists point to the Old Testament's description of God as someone who took a human shape and argued with Abraham and Moses; someone who put out his hand to cover Moses' eyes as he was passing by and only removed it to let him see his backside (Ex. 33:23).

But is there any evidence that any of these writings are true? Why should we believe them to be the divine truth when we know that everything in the Old and New Testaments was written by humans and is tainted by their individual thoughts and interests? Belief in the accuracy of the Scripture requires faith, and the faithful tell us that it is God-inspired. This is not necessarily a fanciful statement since, if there is a God, we would certainly expect that he would try to offer us guidance.

In chapter 8 we will discuss at much greater length the origin of human inspiration and how it essentially corresponds to downloading knowledge from the universe—God, if you prefer. We must keep in mind, however, that we can comprehend new knowledge only as it relates to the knowledge we already have. Would it have been possible for the ancient Hebrews, for instance, to understand the cosmological theories of the Big Bang? Some believe that this gap between truth and that which we are capable of understanding can only be bridged through allegories. You will thus find many faithful who accept the Bible stories as allegories that make important points but that, nevertheless, are not historically true.

On the other hand, we should not ignore the propensity of people to consciously or unconsciously interpret a message in a way that will satisfy their own interests. "God told me to do it," is a defense you occasionally hear in criminal cases. Whether the defendant really believes it and whether he is sane are points to be decided by the jury. We can find in today's nation of Israel an important modern example of using the Bible's contents to justify personal interests. "God gave us this land and it is ours," has been the justification for forcefully ejecting hundreds of thousands of Palestinians from their homes and taking over their land. It is true that the Hebrew Bible does say so; but was that written because God actually said it or in order to defend the ancient takeover of the Canaanite land by the Hebrews who were escaping Egypt?

The fact remains that if you don't have faith in the accuracy of the stories in the Bible there exists no historical reason for believing them; and indeed the majority of the world's population does not believe the Judeo-Christian stories. Many, however, do believe other sacred stories proclaimed by their own religions. Is there any way to objectively discover God?

A friend of mine called me one day to tell me that he had an invisible black cow in his backyard. “If she is invisible, how do you know she is there?” I asked. “Because I’m finding cow dung on the ground,” he answered. “But how do you know that she is black?” I persisted. “Because whenever I think of cows, I think of black cows,” he replied. And this is how gods are born. We discover something in the world that we think could only have been caused by a god and then, having thus proved his existence to our satisfaction, we attribute to him whatever characteristics we believe a god should have.

It has been proposed recently that humans are hard-wired for God. This means that something in our brains biologically predisposes us to believe in the existence of one or more omniscient, omnipotent beings who care for us and who can reward or punish us. I don’t know about the biological part, but it is easy to understand how such beliefs can enter into the malleable minds of the newborn. Although a baby’s actions are restricted to screaming and thrashing uncontrollably, he recognizes that there are huge beings around him who can perform all sorts of wonderful deeds: they can turn dark into light, and the reverse; they can satisfy his hunger and other bodily needs; they can provide comfort, security, and warmth; and, inexplicably, they can also withhold any or all of these.

And as the newborn grows up, it attributes all kinds of superhuman powers to its parents who apparently seem to know everything and can perform all sorts of magical deeds. To a six-month-old its parents are gods. And the feeling persists for a few years. "Mommy, make it well," cries the toddler who scraped his knee. Children, of course, soon learn the limitations of their parents' power; but how much of the early memory of these all-powerful wondrous beings remains in the child's subconscious, ready to be transferred to this new mythical God of his parents?

Many of the so-called logical arguments about God's existence are based on the famous "clockmaker" theory. If you find a clock on the ground you have to conclude that there existed a clockmaker who built it. Its construction is too complicated for it to have come into being by itself. So the early arguments were that the universe is far too complex to have come into existence without outside help. Unfortunately for the theory, modern scientists, including even devout Darwin himself, have been continually discovering "universal laws" that explain the birth and development of the universe as we know it. They have never explained, however, where these "universal laws" originated.

The Modern God

A recent trend in mainline churches is to replace prosaic details with abstract concepts. The concept of love has proven to be particularly attractive and appropriate: "This is my commandment: that you love one another as I have loved you" (John 15:12). By reducing everything to the level of love, many difficult questions can be avoided; even the identity of God. "God is love," pronounced the new pope in his first pontifical encyclical letter. The archbishop of Canterbury agreed, using the very same words. This is not a new idea, however, since it originated in John's first letter (4:8).

But love is an emotion, one that humans and even animals experience, which originates in the paleomammalian brain, not in the cortex, the seat of advanced intelligence. Love, therefore, must be a very basic part of life. It is strangely curious that the noblest thing in the universe unites humans to animals, and apparently to God. But in any case, emotion is a state of feeling; it is not an entity, it is not a being. Although an emotion can affect how an entity reacts, it cannot do anything by itself. An emotion has no consciousness; it is a part of consciousness. An emotion cannot create a universe out of nothing.

It is meaningless, therefore, to say that God is love. One should say, instead, that God loves. This may be true but it still does not tell us what God is. And certainly God does other things besides love. In addition, this also leads us back to an image of God as somebody with a brain; a superhuman. Perhaps the Bible accurately reflects this when it portrays God as saying, "Let us make man in our image." We must conclude that although religion insists on teaching us the word of God, it has absolutely no idea what God is. I don't mean to deprecate the word of God, but many human philosophers have also taught many of the same ideas that we find in the Bible.

Other philosopher/theologians tried a different approach. "God is the ground of all being," declared Paul Tillich. But what does that mean? Forrester Church (in *The Essential Tillich*) explains it this way: "Everything in the world we encounter rests on the ultimate ground of being." God himself "is the ultimate reality. He is the highest being in which everything that we have does exist in the most perfect way." So God is something in which everything exists and out of which everything arises. This describes a combination of what we call "nature" and what (as we will see in chapter 5) Plato called "ideal forms" and Sheldrake labeled "fundamental forms" that serve as templates for the generation of everything that exists in the universe.

The Gnostic Jesus, the presumed creator of the world according to the Gnostic writings not recognized by the church, agreed with this intimate connection between God and the created universe when he said, "It is I who am the All. From me did the All come forth, and unto me did the All extend" (Gospel of Thomas, no. 77); or, "I am the alpha and the omega" (Revelation 22:13, paraphrasing Isaiah 44:6). This kind of God, however, is far different from the one that the Hebrews carried through the desert inside a gold-plated box.

Defining God

Strange as it may seem, I do believe that before we search for God we must define him. This will help direct our search. And I propose that we should search for a God who is pertinent to us, a God who affects us; because a God who does not affect us is irrelevant to us except perhaps in a philosophical way. So I propose that the God we search for should fulfill the following three criteria:

- Our God should be interested in us.
- Our God should be able to affect our existence in this life, or in the next life, if there is one.
- Our God should be able to hear our prayers and entreaties.

Remove any of these requirements, and God's existence becomes immaterial to us. Whether or not he created the universe is of interest only to philosophers and scientists. If he is not interested in us, then he will not bother to interact with us in any manner. If he has no power to affect us in this or the next world, then his existence does not matter. And finally, if he can't hear our prayers, we have no way of reaching him. The importance of this last requirement, however, can be questioned, since there could still be a one-way relationship. He commands and we must follow. That would still render him a relevant God, although not as useful as we would like him to be.

This description of him refers to what people call a "personal God," a God who relates to people. Note that although my description applies to the Judeo-Christian God it is mostly unrelated to his personality and history as described in the Bible. Personally, I am quite comfortable praying to the God of Hebrews and Christians provided that I don't have to visualize him sitting on top of Mount Sinai and inscribing some stone slabs with his commandments for Moses. I almost agree with the heretic Marcion, who in the early second century insisted that the Old Testament was not pertinent to Christian beliefs.

Of the three requirements that I proposed, the only one that is testable is the last one. Does God respond to our prayers? This, however, calls for a more involved discussion and merits a separate chapter or two.

AGNES

MY MOM SAYS, "IF GOD GIVES YOU LEMONS, MAKE LEMONADE"
REALLY.
WELL, I SAY, IF GOD GIVES YOU LEMONS, WHINE ON AND ON ABOUT IT UNTIL HE FINALLY REALIZES THE INJUSTICE AND CAVES IN JUST FOR SOME PEACE AND QUIET!
UM... GOD DOESN'T "CAVE IN," AGNES.
YEAH? WELL THAT'S WHY IT'S SO NOISY DOWN HERE!
8-30
T. COCHRAN

CHAPTER 3

DO PRAYERS WORK?

Religion Says Yes

"Ask and it shall be given to you; seek and you shall find; knock and [the door] will be opened to you," said Jesus (Luke 11:9). What is even more important, he advised us to pray often and unceasingly, illustrating his point with two parables. In the first, someone receives a visitor late at night and, not having any food to offer him, he starts pounding on his neighbor's door asking to borrow some flour. His neighbor is in bed, however, and he refuses to get up. But the pounding continues uninterrupted until he eventually relents and gets out of bed to give his neighbor the flour so he can finally find some rest. In the second parable a widow who has been wronged is asking a judge for justice, but the judge does not want to be bothered and keeps ignoring her. But she makes such a pest of herself that the judge eventually renders a decision in her favor so that he can find some peace. "Will not God, then, avenge his own elect who call to him day and night?" (Luke 18:7).

Christianity is quite clear that God answers our prayers. But science is not so sure. Although a few tests have given positive results, the most recent, large-scale test has literally bombed.

Science Says No

In early 2006, scientists released the results of a painstaking, ten-year long, $2.4 million study of prayer. They selected eighteen hundred people who were about to undergo heart bypass operations and assigned some Roman Catholic monks and nuns, and members of a Missouri prayer link to pray to God for the patients' quick recovery. Prayers were not offered for everybody, however, since some in the test group were kept as controls. Of those prayed for, half were told about it and half were not. To the great glee of atheists the results were clear. According to the newspaper accounts prayers not only did not improve the recovery of the patients but adversely affected it for those who knew that people were praying for them.

It is relatively easy to explain the negative test result on patients in this last group. "I am too sick for doctors to help me so they are calling for prayers," they may have thought. Knowing about the prayers may have triggered what scientists call "performance anxiety," or perhaps an apprehension that doctors expected the worst. Considering what we know today about our ability to mentally make ourselves physically sick, the negative results should have been expected. Even so, why didn't the prayers help the others? Isn't this proof that God, if there is one, does not pay any attention to them? Certainly this was the interpretation that the press presented.

But were the praying groups really entreating God to make these sick people better? If that was the case, they would have prayed on behalf of all the sick, not for only half of them. It is obvious, at least to me, that the purpose of their prayers was not to help the recovery of the ailing but to discover whether God answers prayers, perhaps even to prove or disprove his existence. Yet the Bible, the word of the God to whom they were praying, is clear: "You shall not put the Lord, your God, to the test" (Luke 4:12). Is God really our puppet to perform at our command? Can we quantify and measure his performance? A God who really wanted to convince us of his existence would surely have found many ways to do it during the last millennia. Were the scientists really hoping to outsmart God? Catch him unawares and scientifically prove his existence?

But if God were to intervene in our lives, wouldn't he be breaking the universal laws that he himself established? Not so! Many people, myself included, believe that God answers prayer requests by acting through his own creation and adapting for his purpose the natural laws themselves. Perhaps when we successfully pray to God to heal someone, it is not his direct involvement that accomplishes the task but some yet undiscovered powers in our own human mind activated by our praying. So-called faith-healers are supposed to have such healing powers. But in that case shouldn't this test have disclosed such abilities if they existed among the praying groups?

How could this research have discovered these abilities, however, when mental efforts were directed into thin air? It's like picking up the phone and starting to talk to someone without bothering to first dial the number. The praying groups were given a piece of paper with the first name and the last initial of the person for whom they were supposed to pray: John C., let's say. But there are probably hundreds of Johns that fit this description and perhaps a few John Cs. In comparison, most of the people that Jesus healed were literally physically touched by him. In one case the person seeking healing touched him surreptitiously but Jesus immediately felt it: "Power has gone out of me," he said. Throughout the Church's long history almost every healing, blessing, or power-investing ceremony has taken place through the "laying on of hands."

I imagine that just as a healer places his hands over a particular sick person, so thoughts must be directed towards a specific target. Although there has not been much research in this field, I will venture to

MISTER BOFFO

say that you should not expect to be able to mentally affect someone, in any way, unless you have a very clear idea in your mind of who this someone is. And the experiment discussed above had failed to do that. Certainly a small piece of paper with just a first name and initial on it is not sufficient to identify and direct a mind to one of the six billion inhabitants of this planet.

So a closer look at this research stops me from rushing to discard my belief that prayers are answered. It convinces me, instead, that whatever this experiment may have been intended to prove, it was very badly designed to do it. I must conclude that this study not only wasted a great deal of money but it generated seriously incorrect conclusions. The reader can get more detailed information regarding this test by querying "prayer study" on Google.

Perhaps God does personally intervene to answer our prayers. Literature is full of stories of miraculous cures and rescues. Many how-to books have been written recently claiming to teach the reader how to fulfill his wishes and control his life through properly directed thinking. The great Oprah has even blessed one such book. But one must be careful. Sometimes a prayer is answered in a startlingly unexpected manner.

BIZARRO

Elements rearranged from original artwork to fit page.

CHAPTER 4

PRAYERS AND THE COMPUTER GOD

I asked for strength,
  and God gave me difficulties to make me strong.
I asked for wisdom,
  and God gave me problems to solve.
I asked for prosperity,
  and God gave me brain and brawn to work.
I asked for courage,
  and God gave me danger to overcome.
I asked for love,
  and God gave me troubled people to help.
I asked for favors,
  and God gave me opportunities.

I received nothing I wanted,
  and I received everything I needed.

(From the Internet)

Sometimes, however, the results that prayers bring are not this easy to explain.

A Prayer Gone Awry

My wife's immediate family died when she was one year old. Her father, mother, older sister, a maternal uncle and grandmother were killed on a Pennsylvania highway when their car collided with a truck. She was ejected through the broken windshield and was the only survivor. Fortunately she was promptly adopted and raised by her father's sister whose only son had, coincidentally, just died. As it often happens in accidents where there is a sole survivor, my wife often wondered why she alone had been spared. Perhaps because of this event she had always been terrified of dying.

It is understandable, therefore, that after she experienced a scary cancer episode I prayed deeply that when her time eventually came, death would be swift and unexpected. Defining prayer as an intense soulful request addressed to a metaphysical power, I have not prayed in such a manner more than six times throughout my entire life. This was perhaps the second. A month later my wife died in her sleep. Eventually, the coroner released a death certificate listing the cause of death as "unknown."

Frankly, the event left me shook up. Could I attribute this coincidence to my prayers? Certainly this was not what I thought I was praying for, and yet my prayer was accurately answered. I was granted exactly what I asked for. Although this was not what I had in mind, this was what I had asked for. It is like going to a computer-operated change-making machine, inserting a ten-dollar bill, pressing the "Make Change" button, and having a thousand pennies pour out. That's not what you had in mind, but you asked for change, and you got change. You can't blame the machine. But is God a machine? A computer?

Encountering the Prayer Response Computer

In 1953, on the very day I graduated from college, I decided that I was adult enough to start smoking. So I immediately bought myself a pack of Philip Morris cigarettes and started puffing. By the time I quit in 1968 I was burning through four packages of Pall Mall each day. Giving up smoking was probably the hardest thing I ever did. I remember that I spent the first three months at work just sitting at my desk and thinking how nice it would feel to be smoking. Doubtlessly, if my boss had known about it he would have been thinking how nice it would be if I was working instead. Then suddenly the urge to smoke went away and it never came back again. Except that even now, almost forty years later, I still enjoy the smell when a passerby puffs on his cigarette. And I still dream of smoking. In these dreams I always scold myself for starting to smoke again. “Don’t you remember how difficult it was to give them up?” I tell myself.

Unfortunately, one thing that I substituted for cigarettes during those days was hard liquor. Taking a sip of straight bourbon or scotch provided a burning feeling down my throat that felt almost as good as smoking. And bringing the glass to my mouth closely resembled the same motion with a cigarette. I don’t drink my liquor straight anymore but I still drink it, probably in greater quantities than is good for me. So every now and then I make an effort to give it up. It lasts for two or three weeks but then something always happens to get me off the wagon. So one time, a few years ago, I thought to myself that giving up drinking might be easier, perhaps, if I recruited the aid of prayer. If prayer works, I told myself, why not ask God to help me get rid of my unwanted habit? So I did.

And that introduced one of the strangest periods in my life. In those days my mother was in what proved to be the last days of her life. I had moved her into my bedroom and had relocated myself down to the basement. A nurse took care of her when I was at work and I took over after I came home. If she needed me at nights she could hit the intercom with her cane and I would hear it downstairs and come upstairs. Somewhat coincidentally with my prayer for help with quitting drinking my mother started using her cane vigorously.

BANG, BANG, would go my intercom. I would wake up and go upstairs.

"What do you want, Mom?" I would ask.

"Could I have a glass of water, my son?"

"Sure thing, Mom."

So I would get her some water, and go back to bed. Just as I was starting to fall asleep there would come another BANG, BANG. Back upstairs I would go.

"What is it, Mom?" I would ask.

"Can you please help me to the bathroom, my son?" she would reply.

"Sure thing, Mom."

I'd help her to the bathroom and then bring her back to her bed and return to my own. As I was falling asleep, BANG, BANG would go the intercom. Up the stairs I would go again.

"What is it, Mom?" I would ask.

"What time is it, my son?"

"It's twelve fifteen. Now go to sleep, Mom."

Back downstairs and into bed I'd go. I would be barely asleep when BANG, BANG would wake me up. Back upstairs I would go.

"What would you like, Mom?"

"Is it time to wake up now, my son?"

"No, Mom, see, it's still dark outside."

Back downstairs for me and into bed, but just as I was falling asleep, BANG, BANG would go the intercom sending me upstairs again.

"What is it, Mom," I would ask.

"Can I have a glass of water, my son?"

After a few days, sleep deprivation set in. I felt like these captives who are forbidden to sleep while being vigorously interrogated. I couldn't eat anymore, I couldn't drink anymore, I was sick to my stomach. But my prayers had worked. I had given up drinking; all drinking, booze, coffee, milk, soda, with hardly any conscious effort. After a couple of weeks it became evident that someone was going to go: either my mother or I. Fortunately for me it was her. She went the way she had always wanted to, in her sleep, right after her breakfast.

There was another occasion when I prayed with urgency and strong intent. After twelve years with my company, and after two promotions, I found myself assigned to a different department that had needed my newly acquired computer skills. A few years later people in the department acquired the necessary computer skills, the department was ordered to downsize, and the boss wanted to protect the job of one of his personal friends by reassigning him to my position. It was an ugly story and I will not go into the unpleasant details. My alternatives were to either find another job within the company or to leave. I remember lying in bed at night pushing my thoughts out: "You out there, I can't cope with this; I need help." This took place just before Christmas; in mid-December or so.

Fortunately, in late January my previous boss managed to get me reassigned to his department, something that was not so easy to do with a job freeze in the company; it cost me a double demotion but I kept my salary and growing pension intact. This, of course, is not such an improbable story that requires divine intervention. What makes it unusual is that at the beginning of February I received a call that my mother-in-law had died. This was completely unexpected since she had not mentioned any health problems when I had last talked to her before Christmas. Apparently she had been diagnosed with ulcers a little earlier and just after Christmas the doctors discovered that instead of ulcers she had an incredibly fast-growing stomach cancer; she died within a month.

What is relevant to the story is that she left my daughters a substantial inheritance that would have helped with our immediate financial difficulties if things had not been resolved satisfactorily at work already. Consider the coincidence: I pray for help and almost immediately a process starts that would have provided my family with some financial help if nothing else worked out. Of course, we all die sooner or later; but the timing and unexpectedness of the event is striking. Besides, my mother-in-law was active, young-looking, enjoying life, and appeared as if she would live to reach ninety if not a hundred.

So did my prayers bring about her death? As a reality-centered engineer I can only consider the idea ludicrous. But as a scientist who tries to keep his mind open, I go back to the first chapter of this book and read what I myself wrote there regarding synchronicity: how everything in the world is interconnected and how our actions affect our environment, much like passing speedboats generate waves that rock nearby crafts from side to side.

Is God a Computer?

So every time I pray somebody dies? Shouldn't this be enough reason to turn me off from praying? Frankly, I try to not pray anymore. I say thank you whenever something nice happens but I try to avoid asking for help, which is a shame since I do believe that prayers get answered. As we saw in chapter 3, in Luke's Gospel Jesus advises us to pray often and incessantly until our requests are granted and we finally shut up. Although in those parables Jesus is talking about entreaties to a human judge and to a human neighbor, he is really addressing how we pray to God.

Such reasoning, of course, does not say much about the Judeo-Christian God. Does he really answer our prayers only so that we will stop bothering him? If this is true, then we will have to radically readjust our image of him. But what if the prayer-answering mechanism were an entity like a computer? Such a device has a limited number of access ports, and we would have to keep calling again and again until we got an open line. And when we finally did get through, the computer would search for the easiest way to fulfill the request. “Please, if only I did not have to go to work tomorrow,” we would ask. “Easily done,” the computer would reply, “You are fired.”

This, of course, is not what religion teaches. In my Church we pray: “You, who knows our needs before we ask....” If you want the Church’s point of view ask your pastor for it; here I am stating my personal observations. And these agree with the common maxim, “Beware what you pray for, because you may get it.” If you really feel that you must pray for rain, go ahead and pray. But first buy yourself an inflatable raft and an air pump, just in case God answers your prayer...and answers it...and answers it...and answers it....

Nevertheless, it is obvious that God does not respond to all prayers. If he answers some, why does he ignore others? Since we don’t know anything about God, we cannot really answer this question. Maybe he does answer them all except that sometimes the answer is “No!” But there are other possibilities. Maybe for some reason our prayers are not heard; remember what I said earlier about praying insistently in order to get through? Perhaps there is a proper way to pray. Or maybe answering our prayer would bring evil to someone else. Or perhaps we are praying to ward off something that has already taken place; protect my soldier son, prays his mother, but the boy has already been killed. Finally, some things are unavoidable. No matter how much one prays, a person will eventually die; it is far better to pray for a good life and avoidance of suffering than for an unending life.

Getting back to the discussion about the way God has been answering my prayers, could it be that I have been dealing with his computer? Has God installed an automated answering system like everybody else these days? Is God himself, perhaps, a computer? What is a computer, anyway? It is a man-made device that uses certain operating programs and the information in its database to respond to queries addressed to it. Computers are used to run machines and factories and to forecast the weather, among many other things. A few specially designed machines can vanquish the best human chess players. Many people describe the human brain as a kind of computer; more versatile than any electronic machine but probably of lesser power when performing a single dedicated task.

Although computers possess intelligence they don't possess what we call self-awareness. "I think, therefore I am," said Descartes. In a few years, however, after a little more programming, computers will also be able to think on their own; provided, of course, we keep them plugged in. The next step then will come when they figure out how to stop us from unplugging them, a situation that can lead to extremely bad results as many science fiction authors have described.

NON SEQUITUR

Perhaps this computer-God I am imagining is nothing more than an advanced intelligence that has access to information and can manipulate nature. It does not have to be omniscient or omnipotent. In fact we have already concluded that, if this power exists, it is not omniscient since it cannot divine our true intentions; and we should not expect it to be omnipotent since this would require it to break the laws of nature to which it itself is subject. If you expect me to describe this entity you will be sorely disappointed. But I can describe a "what if" idea that has been postulated by Ronald Lewis Tarter in his short monograph, *The God Theory*.

In that book, Tarter discusses the newest idea in physics, string theory. According to this theory, the basic building blocks of all particles are tiny energy filaments shorter than the smallest knowable dimension in the universe, which vibrate in ten or more dimensions. Hopefully, their existence will eventually explain gravity but that is still decades away and, in any case, of no interest to us here. The author then makes one of these jumps in thinking that introduce new eras in science: just like human intelligence and consciousness result from the interconnections of the billions of neurons in the human brain, so also the interconnections between the trillions of trillions of trillions of submicroscopic vibrating strings in the universe may give rise to a humongous intelligence and consciousness. This he calls God. According to

Tarter, therefore, God is the living consciousness of the universe. It is everywhere and permeates all. This concept is in full agreement with Paul Tillich's statement of faith, "God is the ground of all being."

How much does this consciousness know? How much can it do? But if those strings are the basic constituents of everything, then we also must be composed of them. So God is part of us, and we are part of him. Of course, the existence of these vibrating string entities has not been proven yet, let alone their purported cumulative interactive intelligence. We can thus compare science's description of God as an almost infinite mind to the Judeo-Christian description of God as an anthropomorphic being with infinite powers. You can select whichever you are most comfortable with; neither can be proven and both are probably oversimplifications of something beyond our comprehension. Let us turn our attention now from God to the universe that modern physics reveals.

AGNES

SEE? I PUT OUT MY HAND... I SEE MY HAND... BUT I ONLY SEE IT WITH MY EYES!
WWW.CREATORS.COM
©2003 TONY COCHRAN Dist. By Creators Syndicate
...AND THEN I REALIZE THAT MY EYES ARE STILL ANOTHER PART OF THE ME THAT I'M TRYING TO VERIFY! IT'S AN AMAZING LOGIC LOOP!

WARDBALOON@AOL.COM
ARE YOU EVEN LISTENING TO ME?
I MIGHT BE, BUT I'M NOT SURE IF MY EARS ARE REAL.
3-13
T. COCHRAN

CHAPTER 5

REALITY IS WHAT WE MAKE IT

What is real and what is just a product of your imagination? Is your dream real to you while you are asleep? What about when you wake up? Is your pain real? Is the memory of it real? Is a beautiful sunset real? Is the same sunset real for the blind man standing next to you? Is a hologram real? Is a ghost, should you see one, real? Is an electron real? Is the universe real?

Our awareness of our environment is generated by our mind as it attempts to evaluate the messages that our brain receives from our sensory organs. As the fivefold use of the personal pronoun "our" indicates this is an entirely subjective process. The universe that surrounds us is one thing; the understanding of that universe created by our mind may be something entirely different. We sense a solid, material universe. But matter is energy. And energy is something that completely lacks solidity; something that is normally manipulated mathematically. In this chapter we will discuss some ideas proposed by a few avant-garde physicists, which describe the entire universe as a mathematical construction, a universe where matter is continuously appearing and disappearing, and where consciousness and memory share the same consistency as matter. Yet some of these super-modern ideas can be found as far back as Plato, more than two millennia ago.

Imagination

Have you ever awakened from a particularly vivid dream completely disoriented and had to take a few seconds to convince yourself that you were not really in a faraway place being attacked by alien invaders but safe in your own bed? Then went back to sleep, only to find yourself back again in that faraway place as the dream continued? The human mind is a strange thing. Remove it from outside input and it will construct its own fanciful world.

This is especially noticeable among dementia patients in nursing homes. With many of their memories inaccessible, spending much of their time dozing or asleep, and cut off from much of real life input, they have a hard time telling reality from fantasy. What makes the situation worse is the mind's basic design: it continuously interprets all external and internal inputs in whatever manner will render them consistent with the information remaining in its memory banks so that everything makes sense. Alzheimer's patients often build a completely fanciful world situation around themselves in an effort to explain what their lost memories have rendered incomprehensible.

Once, when I went to visit my father in his nursing home I found him slumped in his wheelchair sobbing uncontrollably.

"What's wrong, Dad?" I asked.

"Oh my son, my son, what have I done to you! I lost all my money and now you are starving in the streets!"

"No, Dad! No one is starving. I'm doing well. I am an engineer, and I have two beautiful daughters. Everyone is doing just fine."

"Aren't you my son the fisherman?" He asked.

It is true that my father had indeed lost all his money, not once but twice. In the old country he had once been a successful businessman, having worked his way through high school and then business school. He had sent his siblings to school, arranged for the marriage of his sister, gave his brothers and brother-in-law jobs in his company, sent his two sons to college in America. Eventually, however, his business succumbed to modern competition by people trained in the American way of advertising and distribution. At the age of sixty he had to turn over all his assets to the tax collector and leave the country for the United States with fifty dollars in his pocket.

In the next twenty-five years he again lived a full life. He opened up two restaurants; he got married three times (twice to the same person), all the while keeping a girlfriend on the side. He helped his sister and his brother back in the old country, gave his two sons down payments to buy their first homes, bought his daughters-in-law new cars. He also arranged for his final retirement at eighty-five. Unfortunately, senility crept in and at the end he made some bad decisions, lost everything he had prepared, and eventually found himself sitting in a mental fog in a wheelchair in a nursing home. Who knows what life this man was now living in his mind.

What, in fact, distinguishes the real world from the ones in our dreams or imagination? "Pinch me to see if I'm awake" does not work because you can do it in your sleep, or at least you think you are doing it. A hallucination seems completely real to a schizophrenic. A monster hiding under the bed appears entirely genuine to a six-year-old. I still remember when I was seven and some strange animal hiding beneath my bed was pushing up on the bed springs. It was real to me then and in my memory it is still real now, so many decades later. But I doubt that the animal was real.

Is the universe in which you live the same as the one in which I live? There is a theory of infinite universes that postulates that every decision that is made creates a fork in history and a new universe. Thus there is a universe where you are reading this book and one in which you are not. According to this theory, therefore, we are all living in universes of our own making. But that probably means that all these universes are imaginary and non-material, since this concept requires the creation of almost infinite mass at every decision instance.

In chapter 6 we will talk about ghosts and other paranormal happenings and discuss whether they really exist or not. But science has set its own rules for separating the real from the imaginary. In order to be considered real, an observation must be reproducible at will under strict laboratory conditions. Since ghosts do not materialize on command, according to science they are not real. Of course scientists often break their own rules when dealing with their own favorite subjects. In particle collision experiments, for instance, scientists may observe a tell-tale ionization path in the gas chamber and announce gleefully: "There goes the mu-meson," or some other particle whose existence they were intent on proving. Scientists first set the rules of the game and then maintain that the game proves that their rules were correct.

Waves and Fields

For healthy normal people, presumably you and me, "real" is whatever interpretation of the world around us is constructed by the filter of our sensory organs, memories, and mind. Some of the input comes through our tactile senses, but whether we experience it as pain or pleasure is a purely subjective matter. Our olfactory organs can recognize a single molecule hiding among a million others to alert our brain to the presence of something identifiable or new. But most of the really exciting input enters our consciousness in the form of waves. Whether it is the sound waves in the air or the electromagnetic waves in the surrounding space, our sensory organs and brain transform them into unique, although essentially arbitrary, constructs.

Consider sound waves, extremely minute pressure variations in the air that can be translated by the ear and brain into something as divine as Beethoven's Ninth Symphony or as earthy as a catfight in the alley. Everybody, however, does not hear the same thing. Few people have the capability, inborn or trained, to tune a piano. Others are deaf and cannot sense airborne pressure variations at all. By the time he wrote his Ninth Symphony Beethoven was completely deaf. At the end of its first performance, which he personally conducted, the orchestra leader had to physically turn him around to face the wildly applauding audience. Yet it is obvious that although he was deaf Beethoven could still imagine the music perfectly in his mind.

Far more important than pressure waves are electromagnetic waves. Depending on their specific frequency we can see them in various colors, we can cook with them, and we can use them to detect faraway airplanes or galaxies. The entire universe remains awash with low-level energy electromagnetic waves, presumably remnants from the Big Bang that brought this universe into being.

Perhaps our most important sense is sight. Electromagnetic waves in a very tiny span of frequencies hit objects around us and bounce off to enter our eyes where they excite the specialized nerves in the retina. These, in turn, generate pulses that travel through a neural network to the brain where in an almost magical way they are transformed into the image of the object. Or, more correctly, into what the brain pictures that object to be.

In my backyard there is a beautiful red maple tree. At ten years old it has not yet reached its eventual maturity, but it is still a joy to see. In the summer its red leaves provide cover for the birds while they wait for an opportunity to raid the bird feeder. At the first noise, squirrels scamper up its trunk for safety. As fall arrives the leaves lose their rich red hues to turn bright yellow, and eventually fall to the ground. Those that pile up around its trunk, on the wildflower bed that my daughter planted, provide cover in the winter to occasional little critters. One year I even saw rabbits nesting there.

But what if I were blind? If I were unable to sense the electromagnetic waves in that tiny frequency range that renders them visible to the eye, would that tree still be there? Yes, I could still walk over and feel its rough bark and reach up and touch the leaves on its branches. But the magic of the colors and the teaming life around it would be lost. Those I would not be able to sense anymore. My world would be different from what it is now.

Einstein established that matter and energy are interchangeable. And physicists argue that subatomic particles are not particles at all but points of concentrated energy. In a way, therefore, the red maple tree in my backyard is not only made visible by energy waves, but is energy. The difference between energy and matter appears to depend more on the human sense apparatus being used than on any intrinsic quality. In a crude way, of course, our Paleolithic ancestors already knew that. You burn wood, you get warmth.

What we call waves, a physicist calls fields. A field is nothing more than a mathematical description of waves that are generated by something. Electromagnetic fields, for instance, describe electromagnetic waves. An interesting thing about fields is that they describe the magnitude and movement of waves everywhere within their applicable range and throughout time. This is something like the kind of knowledge we often attribute to God (omniscience through space and time) but restricted to a single subject area.

Physicists use fields to describe many things besides electromagnetic effects. Gravity fields describe the gravitational effect of masses in the universe, and nuclear force fields do the same for subatomic particles. The most fascinating ones, which are, unfortunately, extremely difficult to describe, are Bohm's implicate order quantum fields.

David Bohm

The physicist David Bohm (1917-1994) was a friend of many of the famous physicists of the 1930s and 1940s, including Einstein and Oppenheimer. Many of them, however, were liberal or outright Communists and his association with them in the 1930s kept him out of the Manhattan Project that developed the atomic bomb during World War II. Ironically, the Ph.D. thesis he was working on during that time at the University of California in Berkeley turned out to be of some importance to that project and so the data in it were immediately classified. He thus lost personal access to his own data, making it impossible for him to defend his own thesis, a very unusual occurrence. After the war ended he was investigated by the McCarthy Committee for Un-American Activities where he claimed the Fifth Amendment so as not to be forced to testify against his former friends. He was prosecuted and, although he was eventually cleared, he was blacklisted out of university circles. As a result he moved to Brazil, then to Israel, and eventually settled in England where he did most of his work.

Bohm was a brilliant physicist who relied upon his intuitive sense to reach conclusions. This by itself is not unusual. Most great scientific advances have been reached intuitively by young men who then spent the rest of their lives trying to justify them; Albert Einstein and Sigmund Freud are well known examples.

Bohm attacked the so-called primacy of the material world: the assumption by both classical and quantum physicists that when we achieve full understanding of everything about space, time, and matter then we will comprehend the universe. He pointed out that all theories are eventually overturned or shown to be valid only within a restricted-parameter value range, something that we should expect if there is more to the universe than we are aware of. He considered consciousness to be a basic, but completely overlooked, constituent of the cosmos.

He also argued against the accepted scientific belief that the total consists of the sum of the parts, which do not interact with each other. He believed that everything is part of a unified whole and that when a part changes, it affects all the other parts. I suppose it is something like looking at two armchairs, four plain chairs, a table, and a sideboard. A scientist would look at the grouping and call it furniture. Bohm would look at it and call it a dining-room set. There may not be much difference until someone replaces a chair with a bed. We still have a group of furniture, but it is not a dining-room set anymore.

Bohm's Universe

Early in the twentieth century, Einstein proposed that the particles forming the visible matter in our universe could be regarded as concentrations in the electromagnetic energy fields that make up this universe. They are real, however, and do react to the external forces to which they are subjected. In the second half of the century David Bohm took this idea a step further. He pronounced matter particles and everything else that we can sense an illusion that he named the "explicate order." He then postulated that this explicate order is enfolded (hidden or coded) into a quantum field that he named the "first implicate order." He insisted that not only are particles and everything else in the universe illusions, but so also is their apparent movement. According to Bohm, this apparent movement results from the rapid appearance and disappearance of particles in adjacent positions, something comparable to looking quickly at successive frames of a movie reel.

Bohm then proceeded to postulate the existence of a "second implicate order," which contains all the rules that control and guide the behavior of the particles generated by the first implicate order. So far this represents a static system. To introduce changes to it he proposed a "third implicate order," which directs the second order and receives input from the first explicate order, the world we see. All this is hard to explain but may be visualized as someone playing a computer game where the explicate and the three implicate orders correspond in ascending order to the picture on the video monitor, the video monitor itself, the computer, and the player who reacts to the picture on the screen thus closing the loop between them.

Bohm used one particular example to explain the interconnectedness of everything in the universe. Pretend that you are looking at a square glass tank where two fish are swimming in perfect synchronization, one towards you and then away from you, and the other from side to side; whenever one changes direction so does the other one also, at the very same instant. It is not fish training, however, that accomplishes this remarkable synchronization, but illusion.

Bohm explains that you are not looking at one real tank that contains two swimming fish but at two superimposed projections of one tank containing one swimming fish, taken by two cameras at right angles to each other. One camera filmed the fish swimming back and forth and the other filmed it swimming to the right and left. Superimpose the two views and you see one tank with two fish apparently swimming in perfect synchronization. It is not an actual physical tank that we are looking at, but an image of one; it is an illusion—and by inference, so is our own universe.

Bohm argued that life's synchronicities (which we discussed in chapter 1) can be explained in a similar manner: our entire universe is an illusion and everything in it is generated by the same type of implicate orders, or fields, to use a simpler term; thus everything is interconnected. But where do you and I fit into all this? Is the observer of the universe part of it? If I am part of my universe, then I must also be part of the illusion; at least my body must be. And since you certainly are part of my universe, you must definitely be an illusion to me. (Let me ask the reader to take another look now at Agnes and her friend in the cartoon at the beginning of this chapter.)

Perhaps the reality of the world around us is no greater than that of an ice sculpture that melts away on the first warm day. There is a story about a child who first listened to a fairy tale on the radio and then watched it on TV. When he was asked which one he liked better he chose the one on the radio. "The colors were brighter," he explained. Does this mean that we create our own world?

Bohm died in 1994, but various other young physicists have followed his reasoning to propose a multitude of equally mind-blowing ideas. Perhaps the simplest of these is the comparison of the universe to a hologram. In order to make a hologram, one takes a picture of an object using split laser beams to produce a film that when illuminated by a laser beam of the original frequency generates in front of it a three-dimensional picture of the object. (An example of such a hologram was the construct of Princess Leah asking for help at the beginning of the 1980 movie *Star Wars*.)

An interesting characteristic of a holographic film is that even a small part of it contains the picture of the entire object, although not with as much clarity. Michael Talbot (in *The Holographic Universe*) suggested that the entire physical universe is nothing more than the reproduction of a mathematical representation. If God created the universe with his mind, then perhaps the universe still remains inside God's mind. And since everything is thus interconnected this also could explain the synchronicity occurrences we discussed previously.

Rupert Sheldrake (in *A New Science of Life: The Hypothesis of Morphic Resonance*) has argued that evolution theory cannot adequately explain the appearance of new species. Using Bohm's terminology he postulated that new life forms, or even new concepts and ideas, result from enfoldments in "generative" (implicate) fields of the third or higher order. He even proposed that great music composers do not invent their own music but download it intact from the universe around them. He quoted Mozart, for instance, as saying that he could see an entire composition in a flash and then he had to either play it or write it down as fast as possible to give it substance.

What is more real then, I ask? The music that comes out of our radio whose volume we can adjust at will or the electromagnetic wave that creates and fills the universe around us, which, once produced, we cannot control? The red maple tree in my backyard or

Bohm's explicate field that he maintains enfolds its form? Science offers us its predictable response: what it can sense is real, and what it cannot sense does not exist. According to science the radio music, its electromagnetic waves, and the maple tree are real; they can all be detected by existing instruments. Bohm's explicate field is not real because no instruments exist yet that can detect it.

Note that in astronomy the size and power of our telescopes determines how far we can see and, therefore, which stars and galaxies we are able to see. Astronomers, however, do not claim that more distant stars and galaxies do not exist just because they are unable to detect them with their current instruments; instead they are constantly building bigger and more powerful telescopes so that they can eventually detect them. Yet scientists don't attempt to build instruments that could detect Bohm's fields.

The sad truth is that established scientists are a conservative, backward-looking group. Very few are willing to spend their time or mar their reputation by investigating apparently outlandish ideas, and even fewer can find sponsors to support them in such endeavors—something necessary since very few modern scientists are independently wealthy. So when science says that something isn't there, it really means that it is currently not visible behind the obstructing curtain of scientific orthodoxy, and that science is not interested in pulling the curtain aside.

CANDORVILLE

FOR EXAMPLE, A FEW BIRDS IN ENGLAND FIGURED OUT HOW TO OPEN MILK BOTTLES. ALL OF A SUDDEN, A HUGE NUMBER OF BIRDS IN OTHER PARTS OF THE COUNTRY FIGURED OUT THE SAME THING.

Elements rearranged from original to fit pages.

Sheldrake argues that his hypothesis explains the observation that soon after someone accomplishes a difficult task many others around the globe suddenly become able to emulate his success. Newly acquired knowledge and skill, it seems, do not remain confined in a single brain but spread out throughout the universe becoming available for "downloading" and discovery. (We should not confuse this, however, with the same phenomenon that is widely observed in the sports world: as soon as somebody achieves the "impossible," many others also accomplish it. In that case it may well be that athletes consciously study and replicate a winner's technique, not to mention the removal of the "impossible goal" psychological block.)

At any rate, Sheldrake argued that once a chemical formulation is compounded for the first time a form or pattern is generated that enables others to reproduce it more easily. We can compare it, perhaps, to crystallization: it is difficult to form the first crystal, but once it is formed other crystals can easily condense on it allowing it to grow quickly (because of the decreased surface energy required). These ideas are very similar, of course, to the "ideal forms" first proposed by Plato more than two millennia ago, where everything in the universe was supposed to be a copy of its perfect representation in heaven.

The computer era provides an everyday example of this process in the preparation of fancy documents. To draw a picture of a butterfly, for instance, I place my clipart disk in the computer, go to the butterflies section, select the picture I like, and insert it on the page where I want it to appear. And there it is; a beautiful picture of a butterfly produced by somebody who can't even draw a decently round simple circle. The only difference being, perhaps, that the clipart was originally presented in a million colors and my printer can reproduce far fewer.

All this sounds like a lot of mumbo jumbo. And perhaps it is. But Bohm's theory may also be an effort to mathematically explain a higher force in our universe, one that many people call God. Seeking God may be similar to looking at a house that a child constructs out of building blocks. When you look at it, do you see a toy house or a child's imagination?

As an example of diverse people thinking the same thoughts, even using the same language, let me conclude this section by quoting from *The Essential David Bohm* (p.119, emphasis added): "Our overall approach has thus brought together questions of the nature of the cosmos, of matter in general, of life, and of consciousness. All of these have been considered to be projections of a common ground. This we may call *the ground of all that is*, at least in so far as this may be sensed and known by us, in our present phase of unfoldment of consciousness." Is it a coincidence that, as we will see in chapter 10, the great modern theologian Paul Tillich defined God as the ground of all being? Or is it one more example that illustrates the growing convergence between modern science and modern theology?

From Plato, to Berkeley, to Bohr

Perhaps the first in the Western world to question the reality of our observations was Plato. In his "*Allegory of the Cave*," in *The Republic*, he asked his friend Glaucon to imagine some criminals who had been chained from birth in a cave, forced to face a wall illuminated by a fire burning behind them. Between the prisoners and the fire was a parapet on which some puppeteers moved puppets around so that their shadows fell on the wall that the criminals faced. Unable to turn and look behind them, these unfortunates assumed that whatever they saw was the real thing, a true representation of similar objects. A shadow of a book, for instance, was what a book really was. Their entire world, apart from each other, consisted only of shadows of real things.

Although the real object of the story lies in what happens when a prisoner removes his chains and leaves the cave, it does not concern us here so we will ignore it. This, however, is where Sheldrake's concept of prototype forms originated, although he talks about copies of the originals, not mere shadows of them. But what kind of originals are they?

Earlier in this chapter I gave an example of copying a picture of a butterfly from a collection of computer clipart CDs. But if you pick up the CD and look at it you will not see any pictures. I did not really copy anything; my computer generated the picture from scratch. It just used information in a number matrix that was encoded on the CD through microscopic changes in the visual properties of its surface. Bohm's followers would argue that just as my picture of the butterfly arose from my computer's manipulation of a mathematical representation, in a similar manner the actual, real butterfly came to being from the unfolding of one of Bohm's explicate fields.

Two millennia after Plato the Irish philosopher-theologian George Berkeley (1685-1753) put forth the theory of "immaterialism" where he denied the independent existence of matter. He argued that we can examine the external world only through our senses. Something can exist, therefore, only while we are observing it; if nobody is observing it, then it ceases to exist. Strange as this idea may seem it coincides with an accepted principle of Niels Bohr's quantum physics: subatomic particles have no properties, or even existence, except when someone is observing them. Berkeley, however, did concede that matter can perhaps exist independently of mankind since God is everywhere and thus can always observe it.

Consciousness

As we saw earlier, Bohm considered that the entire universe, as it appears to us (i.e. the explicate order), is interconnected and arises from the interrelated underlying implicate fields. It follows, therefore, that this interrelationship should also exist between an event and our awareness of that event. Awareness, therefore, or consciousness, as it is often called, must also have its own implicate fields. And since these fields extend and overlap over time, they must give rise to a memory component. Bohm continued on to deduce that matter and mind were connected through a yet higher implicate order. But does this order also allow for their separate existence? Can mind exist when there is no matter? In the next chapter we will examine numerous stories in literature that indicate that this may indeed be true.

THE LOCKHORNS

"LEROY DOESN'T EVEN BELIEVE IN LIFE BEFORE DEATH."

CHAPTER 6

LIFE AFTER DEATH

Old man Qoheleth, in Ecclesiastes, said that only darkness follows death. But how could he know? He had never died and after he did his spirit, if it did survive, did not return to edit his writings. “If there is something after death, why doesn’t somebody come back and tell us?” ask the skeptics. The great Houdini had promised to come and do so but he never came. So did my mother, and she never came, either.

Yet there are thousands of stories of people who insist that relatives or friends appeared to them after their death. The most famous instance of this in literature is the appearance of the resurrected Jesus to his disciples. It follows that all Christians must automatically believe in life after death; but what of non-Christian? Even the most cursory look at published literature will reveal thousands of reported stories of what, for lack of a better word, we call ghosts or apparitions of dead people. Were all the people who reported these sightings, delusional?

A Goodbye

One night, three or four weeks after my wife's death, I felt a little tired and went to bed early. Just as I was falling asleep and was in that twilight period between sleep and wakefulness, I sensed her coming in the room, sitting at the edge of the bed and resting her hand on my shoulder; just as she had done on many past occasions when feeling a little sick or tired I had retired early. For a few seconds it seemed as if I was being enveloped by an almost tangible feeling of goodbye, strangely filled with sadness and a mental message, "I feel so sorry for all the things you have to go through," that somehow seemed to be associated with the task of raising our two young daughters by myself. I started to sit up and put my arm around her, but my hand went right through her body, and she disappeared as I instantly became wide awake.

According to researchers, almost one-third of widows and widowers report at least one, but no more than three, ghostly encounters with their dead spouses. Because these encounters are almost always structured as "goodbye events," psychologists attribute them to the survivor's need to properly take leave of his or her spouse, especially in cases where the death was sudden and unexpected. They have named them, therefore, grief-induced hallucinations.

Although this explanation certainly fits my situation it does not explain the emotion of almost pity that was expressed, something that I never felt for myself either then or at any time since, and that was never justified by any future events. Scientists also argue that since these appearance events are so common and predictable, they must be false. I find this last argument to be the exact opposite of what one would normally assume: that the more often something is observed the greater the probability that it really exists, not the reverse.

Science does not accept the existence of ghosts or similar hallucinations, mostly because their occurrence does not meet the accepted rules of science: an event can be considered to be real only if it can be reliably reproduced in a laboratory environment. Ghosts, like all other paranormal phenomena, do not satisfy this criterion. Yet there are thousands upon thousands of stories that involve ghosts or some kind of communication from the dead. Certainly there is far more evidence for the existence of ghosts than for the existence of the various gods postulated by the world's many religions. Yet many devout believers consider gods to be real and ghosts figments of imagination.

Ghosts

I will venture to say that despite science's disbelief, half of the people in this country will either see a ghost within their lifetime or talk to a person they trust who has seen one. Ghost apparitions fall in various groups. We have already discussed one of them, the "goodbye" kind. Many of this "goodbye" type of apparitions, however, serve another purpose as well: to reassure the living that the one who has just died is doing all right in his new world.

Another type of apparition is the "I'm keeping an eye on you" type. It usually involves a loved one who appears during important events: it can be the birth of a grandchild, the wedding of a daughter, or a timely warning that prevents an accident. In all these cases someone recently dead appears to one who is either celebrating a happy event or is in danger. None of these appearances can be objectively substantiated, so their acceptance is based only on the testimony of the persons involved. Yet published literature is full of such stories.

In a similar type of apparition, a dying person reportedly sees in the last minutes of his life a dead relative standing near his deathbed; presumably to assist him to cross over. Of course, nobody else can see him. Interestingly, a policeman recounted on the Internet a related observation: "I've seen many dying people acknowledge the presence of dead relatives by their deathbeds, but I have never encountered it in cases of sudden, accidental deaths," he wrote. Perhaps time and travel limitations exist even in the next world.

In a "crisis apparition," someone who just died in an accident appears to a loved one or to someone who is in a position to help others still at the accident scene. In this category belong all the stories of people who sensed the death of a person at the exact time when it happened or saw the person's ghost at that same instant. Many people who report such occurrences insist that it was later established that the ghost appeared to them in the same clothes that he was wearing at the moment of his death, or that he exhibited evidence of the wounds that caused his death. Because, however, such events occur at the exact time of the other person's death they can also be interpreted as the result of a telepathic message from the dying, but not yet dead, person.

"Recurring apparitions" involve ghosts who perform the same repeated actions over and over at the same location and are visible to many people. You find stories of such ghosts in descriptions of castles, battlefields, or haunted houses. They are almost always associated with gruesome events. One proposed explanation is that the surroundings have been imprinted by the psychic energy of the event and the ghostly vision is comparable to a tape recorder playing the same segment over and over. Another explanation is that the dead person is unaware of his death and is stuck inside a time loop.

"Poltergeist activity" generally describes paranormal events occurring at a specific location and involving moving or flying objects, opening and closing of doors and windows, or banging and other unexplained noises. Many of these events have been substantiated by police and scientists. In some cases the occurrences were associated with young persons who were present while these events were taking places and who presumably were causing them unconsciously with paranormal psychic powers. Removing them from the premises stopped the paranormal activity. In other cases, the source was attributed to a dead person who had lived or frequented that location during his life and who was unaware that he was now dead and was unhappy with the new people who had moved into what he considered to be his personal space. Such spirits are usually either exorcised away or talked into moving on.

The real existence of ghosts assumes, of course, that something survives physical death. I will follow the usual convention and call this surviving element the soul, and I will discuss this at greater length in the next chapter. First, however, let us turn our attention to another paranormal event that has gained much attention in the last three decades.

Near-Death Experiences

In 1975 Dr. Raymond Moody published an extraordinary book, *Life after Life*, in which he described stories recounted to him by people who had come very close to death and who, occasionally, had even been pronounced dead by attending physicians. In the following ten to fifteen years additional books were published with similar stories, which claimed to corroborate his findings. Let me summarize the more common aspects of these accounts for those readers who may still be unaware of this phenomenon.

A person may be on a hospital operating table or sound asleep in bed when he sees a bright light shine upon him and hears a voice emanating from it saying, "Come, come." The person then feels himself rising from the laid-out position and moving toward the ceiling from where he can look down at his own physical body and any people around it, and even hear their conversations. Sometimes the experience ends at this point with the disembodied person getting scared and jumping back to merge with his physical body.

At other times, however, the disembodied person zooms up through a dark tunnel into a world where everything is bright and where there are no shadows. Complete lack of shadows is a distinctive and consistently described feature of this world. There, he is usually met by an authority figure occasionally identified as Jesus, Moses, or one's grandfather. He often sees his dead relatives, all of them emanating light and casting no shadows, but he never interacts with them. Sometimes the person stands in judgment of his entire life as it passes in review in front of him but, interestingly, it never involves an external judge. Occasionally he is given explanations about the workings of

BIZARRO

Elements rearranged from original artwork to fit page.

the entire universe although he always forgets them when he returns to his physical body. Many people find this place so full of happiness that they want to remain there forever. They are told, however, that their time has not come yet and suddenly find themselves back into their actual body, conscious again of the physical pain caused by the accident or operation that had precipitated this occurrence.

Such an experience almost always changes a person's life, rendering him more spiritual and less attracted to formal religions; these groups, by the way, almost invariably discount the reality of the episode. Some people report that they have gone through repeated near-death experiences. Unfortunately, there are also occasions where some young people later try to commit suicide in an attempt to return to this heavenly place. Scientists, of course, do not accept the authenticity of these events but attribute them to chemical changes in the brain, induced either by oxygen deprivation or the release of stress-related endorphins. On the other hand, some people maintain that they can consciously attain and control somewhat similar out-of-body experiences and that they can travel around at will in their so-called spiritual bodies.

The first reported case of a near-death experience appears in Plato's *Republic.* Paul also described such an incident, saying that the person involved was carried to the third heaven where he heard many wonderful things, but Paul insisted that he was not referring to himself. Personally, I doubt this last assertion because I believe that only such a momentous event would explain the sudden and complete change in Paul's personality and beliefs. Finally, on a personal note, I should add that my wife experienced the abbreviated version of such an event a couple of weeks before her death. Although she was not aware of its meaning, I was, but I did not voice any thoughts about it.

Communications with the Dead

Contacting the spirits of the dead was an ancient practice but strictly forbidden by the Hebrew God. "Do not go to mediums or consult fortune tellers," admonishes Leviticus (19:31), although later King Saul has the spirit of Samuel conjured up to give him advice. People have probably attempted to talk to their dead relatives since the dawn of history but it became particularly popular during the nineteenth century when presumably talented mediums were used as intermediaries. That was a period when much serious psychic research was done, especially in England. Unfortunately, so many of the mediums turned out to be frauds or outright crooks that the entire field became tainted and abandoned.

In recent years Dr. Gary Schwartz, a professor at the University of Arizona, has attempted to perform meticulous scientific studies to prove that some talented mediums are capable of contacting spirits of dead persons. He described his work in great detail in *The Afterlife Experiments*, a very interesting book for those who are interested in how the medium business works. Nevertheless, I remain unconvinced about his conclusions because I believe that all his findings can be easier explained by attributing telepathic abilities to the mediums who participated in his experiments. Of course, even proving the presence of such telepathic abilities would represent a significant finding since science does not accept the existence of telepathy any more than it accepts the existence of spirits.

Personally, I don't feel comfortable using the work of mediums to prove the survival of the soul; there are too many factors that cannot be controlled. Nevertheless I do believe that the huge number of unexplained spirit-stories cannot be conveniently ignored. Where there is smoke there may be fire, and if even only one ghost story out of the thousands recorded is true, it is still sufficient to prove the existence of spirits. But can anything really survive physical death, and if so, what?

MISTER BOFFO

Reprinted by permission of Joe Martin.

Elements rearranged from original artwork.

CHAPTER 7

BRAIN, MIND, AND SOUL

People usually have two main objections when rejecting the idea that anything survives physical death: where is the proof, and what is it that survives? We dealt with the first objection in chapter 6. Here we will seek the identity of the survivor, defined as the "soul," and discuss the confusion that has arisen in the last 2,600 years between the terms "soul" and "spirit." Then we will search for the location in the body of the decision making and control centers of the individual, and see how these relate to his conscious and unconscious. Here we will encounter the latest revolutionary theories regarding the complete subordination of the conscious to the unconscious: how the unconscious makes all decisions and the conscious serves only to justify them.

This will lead us to the source of a person's individuality, the memory. There are two possibilities regarding its location: the accepted theory postulates that memory is generated by the interconnections between the neurons in the brain, which rules out the memory's after-life existence; a new, far-out hypothesis, on the other hand, places the memory outside the confines of the physical body, thus enabling it to survive physical death. This rather strange hypothesis is supported by Bohm's quantum field theory where matter is just a mathematical manifestation and by Talbot's holographic universe concept where everything is interconnected—both theories were discussed in chapter 5. I will conclude with the proposition of an energy entity (some might prefer the adjective "spiritual") that contains a person's memory and survives physical death.

Definitions

As with so many other things, it all started with the ancient Greeks. They postulated that two distinct non-material entities were attached to the body: psyche (soul, mind) and pnevma (nous, spirit). The psyche was supposed to direct the body's operations, keep the body alive and eventually die with it. This corresponds to what we now call mind. The pnevma (most people erroneously spell it pneuma) represented an entity that survived physical death and was a special, divine creation.

Paul continued with this concept comparing our earthbound "psychic" body with our future "pnevmatic" body (Cor. 15:45). These assumptions agree with our current nomenclature: doctors who specialize in the working of the mind are called psychiatrists, and mediums who claim that they can contact the spirits of dead people are called spiritualists. The *Holmes Bible Dictionary* also agrees, defining "soul" as the body's life principle; when it dies, so does the body. Something, perhaps, like the Energizer, the Eveready rabbit's battery shown on TV: when the charge is used up the rabbit stops moving; except, of course, that this never happens in the commercials.

In the Synoptic Gospels, however, (those written by Mark, Matthew, and Luke) the words "soul" and "spirit" were used interchangeably, and in John's Gospel the word "spirit" was associated almost exclusively with the Holy Spirit. Modern nomenclature has continued the confusion. These days the "soul" is identified as the entity that survives death and possibly goes to heaven or hell, and the word "spirit" is used to refer to ghostly apparitions, materializations of the soul. Continuing with the definitions, everybody agrees that the "brain" is the visible and palpable gray matter inside our heads, which operates much like the computer hardware used to run machines or even entire factories. And the word "mind" is increasingly used to describe the operation of the brain. The word "psyche" has fallen into disuse.

Not everybody agrees with these definitions, but proper communication requires only that the hearer knows what the speaker means when he uses a particular word. So here I am making it clear that I am using the word "soul" to describe a nonphysical, energy entity that contains identifying information and knowledge about the physical body to which it was once connected, which survives the destruction of that body to continue an independent existence. Notice that I am using the word "energy," not "spirit," because we all know what energy is, but there is a wide disagreement regarding what "spirit" is.

The existence of this "soul" is not a proven fact but, as you will know from the previous chapter's discussion, I believe in its reality. Now I will try to describe one way the soul's existence can be scientifically explained, keeping in mind, of course, that it is only the result of a "what if" thought process.

Memory

Although we are all human, each one of us is mentally unique. We all have our own likes and dislikes, our individual strengths and weaknesses, and especially our unique memories. Even identical twins that have grown up together possess distinctly different memories. In the end it is our memories that make each one of us unique. And when dementia attacks and destroys our memories, then we cease being who we were and become just flesh-and-blood machines.

It seems reasonable to conclude that if my soul is to survive my physical death it must, at a minimum, possess my memories. Likes, dislikes, talents, and other individual features are not necessary because these may change even during my life. Sinners turn into saints, patient parents become cranky grandparents, timid followers become fearless leaders or, of course, the reverse. And what about the souls of Alzheimer's patients? you may ask. I once thought that they remained deficient, and I had even composed a parable to bemoan the dangers of unnecessary life prolongation. But as you will see below, I feel there is a better answer.

Scientists have made remarkable progress in their understanding of the physical brain and believe that they know how it works. They tell us that as animals evolved into increasingly more intricate life forms, nature developed increasingly more complex brain structures for their use. But not wanting to waste past development work, instead of replacing the inferior brain with the superior, nature just placed the new brain around the old one. Its final achievement, the neo-mammalian brain, is represented by the huge expanse of the cortex, which contains one hundred billion interconnected little neurons that pass messages to each other through electrochemical means. Mankind's intellectual dominance over other mammalian species is thus based on the larger and more intricate structure of its cortex.

Memory is nothing other than a record of past brain activities. All the conscious information that enters the brain and all the conscious thinking and decision-making performed by the brain goes into memory. According to scientists, memory is encoded in the specific interconnections of the brain neurons. However, it is not located there in specific locations like files in a file cabinet but is spread throughout the entire cortex mass in a manner similar to the holograms we discussed in chapter 5. Consequently, physical destruction of a part of one's cortex will not necessarily destroy a part of the memory. But even if some memory were lost it could, and often does, eventually return.

Seemingly opposing this view, however, is the reported discovery that when an electrode touches certain specific locations of the brain mass it elicits the detailed replaying of past events, complete with their original sight, sound, and smell contents. And even though these events might have been completely forgotten by the subject they are remembered in exactly the same manner whenever the identical points of the brain are stimulated. (Strangely, for some unknown reason, this finding is valid only for people suffering from epilepsy; it is also based on fairly old experiments.)

And here lies the main argument against the survival of souls. I specified that a soul contains one's memories. But if these memories are located in the brain they must disappear when death destroys the brain structure, and nothing remains to survive. According to currently accepted scientific knowledge, therefore, there cannot be such thing as a soul (as I defined it) and one's individuality does not survive one's death. It is conceivable, however, that accepted science could be wrong. Formerly established scientific knowledge has often been superceded by newer scientific understanding. For instance, the original unbreakable atom of the Greeks was replaced by Bohr's miniature solar system with little spherical electrons supposedly revolving around a large fixed nucleus, which, in turn, was later replaced by mathematical expressions and concepts understood only by the scientific elite.

Memory Fields

Let us now return to our earlier subject of fields. Remember that brain action results from electrochemical signals exchanged between neurons, an activity that is directly observable with modern scientific instruments. You go to your doctor's office, he attaches some electrodes to your scalp and takes an electroencephalogram, a record of your brain waves. In theory, if he had sufficiently sensitive instruments he would not have to make any direct connections but could have measured the electromagnetic waves as they radiated from your head.

Brain activity consists of interactions between neurons. These originate from sensory inputs, and result in conscious and unconscious thoughts and commands sent out to body muscles. Memory is just a record of all this information. And since all neuron interactions generate electromagnetic waves, it follows that we are continuously transmitting outwards instantaneous images, or records, of our memory, records that can be described through mathematical memory fields.

Electromagnetic waves and fields do not attenuate with time like sound waves do, although they do become fainter as they spread out over an increasingly larger spherical domain. (Astronomers, for instance, can observe today nova explosions that occurred 8 billion years ago in faraway galaxies.) So, according to this concept, our past, present, and future thoughts will be floating out there in the cosmos forever. But in the holographic-type universe of modern physics there are no distance limitations, and in Bohm's implicate field theory there are no time restrictions. So in theory, everything, everywhere, anytime, exists here and now without any diminution. God may not be omnipotent but if he can decipher these fields he may be close to being omniscient.

The Brain

Consider something more down to earth, like your radio. Turn your radio on and tune it to a particular station. Get another radio, turn it on and tune it also to the same station. Both radios play the same music and carry the same announcer's voice. Now open the radios and look inside. You see a bunch of wires and electronic parts, probably quite different in each set. Yet both radios sound the same. Take a hammer and smash one of them. It stops playing; the other one, however, continues on. It is obvious that the music is not located inside the radio but in the electromagnetic waves it senses. The radio is just a tuning and amplifying machine. Somewhere in the world there is a transmitting machine that generates the waves that your radio captures.

Is it possible, as some people have suggested, that the brain is a combination transmitter/receiver tuned to a specific frequency, simultaneously generating and receiving memory waves? Is it possible that the brain does not really store memories but just places them into fields around it from where they can be retrieved at will?

Such a possibility is consistent with physical observations and leads to some interesting conclusions. Continuing with the radio broadcast analogy this idea assumes that each physical brain is tuned to a specific wave frequency, so each memory remains unique to that individual. But if some individuals could tune their brains to other frequencies, at will or accidentally, then they would be able to read someone else's thoughts—telepathy.

When a brain becomes damaged and loses its ability to access some parts of its memory field, an observer may assume that its memories have been destroyed. But as the brain mends itself and can again retrieve its lost memories, they magically reappear. So, although the Alzheimer's patient whose brain is destroyed loses access to his memories, the memories themselves continue to exist in space, stored away in their own memory field. When he dies his memories will be intact and his soul whole.

Bernard Haisch proposes in *The God Theory* that the brain not only analyzes information from its environment but also serves to filter out much available information. What we sense about our environment, he maintains, is only a small select portion of what exists out there. We will discuss this idea further in the section dealing with idiots savant.

Reincarnation

This hypothesis also explains why some people report memories of past lives, giving rise to beliefs in reincarnation. The theory of external memory fields suggests that they are just accessing dead people's memory fields and confusing them with their own. The most reliable reported cases of reincarnation involve either young children who identify with a recently deceased person or adults placed under hypnosis. Significantly, in all cases involving young children the foreign memories seemingly disappeared by age ten.

One possible explanation for the children's foreign memories is based on two presumptions: first, the children have not developed yet proper control of their memory process; and second, there exist nearby memory entities released from people who have just died, which may have not realized yet their new independent status and so do not block outside access to them. Notice that the surviving memories I am discussing here consist not only of a passive repositories of information but also of active operating processes. They are thus similar to computer memories, which contain both data and operating programs. Is it then also possible that the surviving souls, not being encumbered by physical limitations, have greater capabilities than the earthbound minds did? We will continue some of this discussion in the next section.

The cases in which adults apparently retrieved foreign memories while under hypnosis may be directly related to the way hypnosis affects one's brain control or imbues it with greater abilities. It is well known, after all, that under hypnosis people are capable of doing many things that they normally cannot do when fully conscious.

But how is it possible for someone to confuse something real with something imaginary? Events that happened with events that were only imagined? The explanation lies in the fact that the brain accepts all memories as true unless it remembers how it acquired them. It follows that someone who has access to the memories of Marie Antoinette would automatically assume that she actually is Marie Antoinette. And since this is obviously untrue, she can only assume that she had been Marie Antoinette in the past and that she is now living as a different incarnation.

The Conscious

At the beginning of the chapter I defined one's soul as consisting, at the very least, of one's memories. And I argued that memories are electromagnetic energy and thus exist forever. Still earlier we had discussed how matter and the entire universe are energy. So we have now traced a full circle. The matter in our physical bodies consists of "materialized" energy. Upon our physical death the energy associated with our physical body disintegrates into basic molecules, but our memories and other brain activity continue to exist as free energy in the universe. In this manner the soul that was created while we were in the womb and that matured as we grew up, survives our physical death. But is this soul conscious?

There is no universally accepted definition of consciousness. For our purposes, however, we can define it as an entity's ability to sense and react to its environment. Our physical brain, for example, is informed by our body's sensory circuits of external events, analyzes its interpretation of the events for relevancy, and then orders an appropriate response by activating the neurons that control physical activity. If an energy entity, then, such as the soul, were conscious, how would it sense the red maple in my backyard? The obvious way would be for it to sample the electromagnetic radiation that bounces off the tree, just as the eye does. But would this energy entity have to follow the procedure the brain does or could it analyze it directly? I don't know.

On the other hand, since the tree is made up of "materialized" energy, it may be directly visible to a conscious energy entity. Eastern mystics maintain that every living thing is surrounded by an energy field, which they call astral aura, that displays the condition of its physical and mental health. These mystics also maintain that one or more of these energy fields are attached to every physical human being and that they separate from the body only upon death or during out-of-body experiences. Perhaps, but I don't know—I am an engineer not a mystic.

Interestingly, blind people who have had out-of-body experiences have reported being able to see during such events. But according to Kenneth Ring and Sharon Cooper (*Mindsight*), it is a different type of sight: "They are able to perceive from all angles at once, from every focal depth at once, [with] a sense of 'knowing' the subject, not just visually, but with a deep and inexplicable knowledge."

But even if we were to agree that the soul has memories, from where does its independent status originate? After all, my computer also has memory but it can only access it when the program it runs directs it to do it. Where does the soul find its program? Just as is the case with the computer, the soul finds the program in its memory. So if the soul contains an individual's memory, then it also contains the program that permits it to act.

Consider the soul of a recently deceased grandmother discovering that she has a new grandchild and deciding to go visit it. The grandmother's soul's program would be something like this: has anything recently happened to those about whom I care? Information comes back saying that a new member has arrived to her still earthbound family. The soul thinks, "I love my family, I wonder what the baby looks like and how everybody else is—let's go see." The program is identical to what it would have been if the grandmother were not dead but lived in a different city. The only difference is the transportation arrangements.

In Bohm's nomenclature the conscious belongs to the third generative/implicate field, the player of the video game we discussed in chapter 5. When we are alive our conscious is directing our brain neurons to run the program; when we are dead it may be activating the vibrating energy strings that we postulated form the consciousness of God. This means that the soul and God are formed of the same material! This is not a new idea: Ralph Waldo Emerson wrote in 1836, "The current of the Universal Being circulates through me. I am part or particle of God" ("Essay on Nature").

If I had chosen to take a spiritualist's approach instead of a scientist's in this book, I would have talked about astral bodies rather than about implicate fields.

If I had followed Christian beliefs I would have discussed Paul's ideas: "It is sown a natural body, it is raised a spiritual body. There is a natural body and there is a spiritual body...the first human Adam was made a living physical body, the final Adam will be raised a living spirit" (1 Cor 15:44-47). But chances are that in all cases I would have reached the same conclusions, since they all involve energy fields.

The Unconscious

Although scientists brag about how well they understand the mind, nobody says much about the unconscious, or subconscious, as it is also called. Yet that is where most of the real work of keeping the body alive is done. The mind is like an iceberg. The conscious part of the mind is what is visible above the water line and its unconscious what is hidden below. The unconscious part of the brain runs most of the automated operations of the body or repeatable segments of learned tasks. It controls what memories we can access, works on solving our problems while we are otherwise occupied, entertains us with dreams at night, and controls our likes and dislikes during the day. But the unconscious probably does much more. In his *Strangers to Ourselves*, Timothy Wilson discusses some experiments that attempted to measure the interval between the time we become aware of something and when we start responding to it. Astonishingly, this time interval turns out to be

GET FUZZY

BOBBIE, the WONDER DOG of OREGON

10/3

FROM AUGUST, 1923, TO FEBRUARY, 1924, A SCOTCH COLLIE - ENGLISH SHEPHERD MIX NAMED BOBBIE MADE PERHAPS THE MOST INCREDIBLE DOCUMENTED JOURNEY TO RETURN HOME. WHILE VISITING INDIANA, BOBBIE WAS CHASED AWAY FROM HIS OWNERS BY A PACK OF LOCAL DOGS. AFTER 3 WEEKS OF SEARCHING, HIS FAMILY WAS FORCED TO RETURN TO OREGON WITHOUT HIM, BROKEN-HEARTED. EXACTLY 6 MONTHS LATER, BOBBIE WALKED BACK INTO HIS HOMETOWN OF SILVERTON, OREGON, TIRED AND EMACIATED. HE HAD TRAVELED SOMEWHERE AROUND 3,000 MILES ON FOOT - THROUGH ICY RIVERS, SNOW STORMS AND OVER HUGE MOUNTAIN RANGES. AS HIS STORY BECAME KNOWN, HIS OWNERS RECEIVED MANY LETTERS FROM PEOPLE WHO HAD SEEN AND/OR HELPED BOBBIE ALONG HIS CROSS COUNTRY JOURNEY.

darb

negative. Apparently we start responding to cues before we even become consciously aware of them. Wilson argues that this indicates that most of our decisions are reached by our unconscious. Furthermore, he maintains that much of our learning bypasses our conscious and is stored directly in areas normally accessed only by the unconscious. So according to Wilson, the unconscious not only responds to the sensory inputs but does it on the basis of information not known by the conscious mind; our conscious minds serve only to manufacture justifications to explain our actions to ourselves.

Working with dreams, Carl Jung concluded that all humankind shares a great deal of information through an unconscious collective memory. He made no attempt to explain how this can physically take place, but we can easily see how well it fits with the theory of external memory. Apparently some parts of this collective memory can be accessed by all, even though only unconsciously. This fits well with Sheldrake's theory discussed in chapter 5, which proposes that knowledge and ideas spread out unconsciously throughout the universe and are available to all seekers. But is there any evidence to justify this external memory theory?

Idiots Savant

"Idiots savant" is a term applied to a small group of people who are either born with, or have suffered, brain damage, who are usually untrainable and have an IQ below 70, but who exhibit extraordinary skills in some specific field: usually lightning-fast mathematical calculations, calendar skills, musical memory, or mechanical/spatial skills. Some exhibit incredible memory, able to memorize at will the entire contents of telephone books. Others can multiply large numbers in their heads, not by following any specific procedure but by watching in their minds the numbers change into the final answer. Some can calculate which day of the week corresponds to any arbitrary date in the next 40,000 years. A few can listen to a piano piece once and repeat it perfectly even though they have never had any piano lessons. (I am quoting this statement here as it is presented in the literature. But I fail to understand how an untrained person, however talented, can play a complicated piece on the piano when this requires so many physical as well as mental skills.)

Where does all this knowledge come from? Where is all the read material stored, and from where is it later retrieved? What permits such superhuman feats in one narrow field when the rest of the brain operates at the level of a three-year-old? As I mentioned earlier, Bernard Haisch proposed in *The God Theory* that the brain acts as a filter that prevents much external information from reaching us. Is it possible that sometimes, when it is damaged, this filter breaks down and the brain opens up to freely receive external memories and information? Is Sheldrake (and others like Plato before him) right when he postulates that all knowledge exists in the universe around us ready to be plucked? Is our mind a little sub-segment of God's mind that we can sometimes access?

• • •

At the start of this chapter we discussed how the ancients believed that a person consisted of three parts in one: the body, the psyche, and the spirit. Even today many believe that a person is made up of the body, the mind, and the soul, although many others disagree about the reality of the soul. The science of taking care of the body is called medicine, and is practiced by doctors. Taking care of the mind is called psychology, which most people think is more of an art than a science, and is practiced by psychologists and psychiatrists. Finally the care of the soul is called religion, and nobody thinks it even resembles science.

Nevertheless, religion has been with us since the dawn of civilization and is currently practiced by pastors or priests. In ancient times, and also in modern era tribal societies, witch-doctors combined all three functions (medicine, psychology, religion) to physically cure people by convincing their minds of religion's potency. We can see a modern version of this practice when we gather at the church to pray for a miracle. Religion has always had a very strong influence in humanity. It is active even in today's secular society masquerading as scientism: "Doctor, please make my kid well," we plead. Let us now turn our attention to religion, specifically the Judeo-Christian religion.

AGNES

IT IS A SIMPLE FACT: YOU DON'T FIND GOOD IDEAS... GOOD IDEAS FIND YOU!
REALLY.
wordbaloon@aol.com

OH, YES... GREAT IDEAS ARE LIKE RADIO WAVES IN THE COSMOS. I JUST HAVE TO TUNE MY MIND IN TO ACCESS THE IDEAS.
©2002 TONY COCHRAN Dist. By Creators Syndicate
www.creators.com

HOOO... HERE IT COMES... A LITTLE MORE... UH-HUH... HUP HUP... WHOOPS! DARN! I LOST THE SIGNAL AGAIN.
THE KNOB MUST BE IN THAT BOWL OF CHEEZ-KURLS.
5-6

CHAPTER 8

RELIGION AND INSPIRATION

What is the source of ideas and inspirations? We do know that they originate in our unconscious, but how? Did Mozart, for instance, order his unconscious to prepare a symphony for him and in due time a symphony flowed ready-made into his conscious mind? If so, where did his unconscious find it or where did it download it from? In the previous chapter we looked at various modern philosophical and scientific theories that suggest all knowledge exists "out there" and that under the proper conditions this knowledge can be unconsciously accessed by our minds. According to these theories inspirations consist of ideas that seemingly pop into our minds out of empty air. If we were to transfer this concept into the realm of religion we would say that inspired religion consists of teachings seemingly sent unbidden by God into the minds of prophets. Actual religion differs from this because it manipulates the teachings to promote a particular group's interests.

The Judeo-Christian writings do not represent unvarnished historical facts but are inspired stories designed to teach the reader; stories that were often derived from memories of past events or well-known myths. But inspiration is not error-proof and we should not expect the holy writings to be completely and literally correct. We will then look at religion's appeal to the faithful: how justice meted out in the next world will make up for the injustices suffered in this world. And we will end on a somber note: the wide gap between organized religion and God's word.

Truth and the Bible

In the Gospel of John, Jesus tells Roman prefect Pontius Pilate that he came to this world to bear witness to the truth and that all who are friends of the truth listen to his voice. To which Pilate responds, "What is truth?" The truth is that this exchange, almost certainly, never took place. History tells us that Pilate was a barbaric man of action, not a philosopher interested in such matters as the truth. Besides, how would John have known about the conversation anyway? Pilate did not write an autobiography.

In fact, all the events of the Holy Week are of dubious historical accuracy, corresponding uncannily to the Book of Zechariah's account of the events that he expected would precede the arrival of the Messianic kingdom. In my previous book I discussed the idea that Jesus, a mystic Galilean revolutionary, consciously carried out the events that Zechariah had predicted, in order to force the fulfillment of the prophecy.

It is also possible, however, that it was the evangelists who purposefully copied the events from the Book of Zechariah, not Jesus. Favoring this argument is Matthew's depiction of Jesus entering Jerusalem riding on both a donkey *and* a colt. Matthew, you see, could not read Hebrew and used the Septuagint, the Greek translation of the Hebrew writings, as a source. And the Greek translators had apparently ignored the Hebrew poetic style of writing in which a verse is immediately repeated with a minor alteration, and produced this strange translation that Matthew copied verbatim. But if Matthew had depended on the Book of Zechariah for his information then he was obviously not recording actual facts.

This is not the only objection that readers have regarding the books of the New and the Old Testaments; they are both full of events that flout all laws of physics. How did Jesus walk on water? How did he heal someone who had been blind from birth? How did Jonah spend three days in the belly of a whale? Some people ignore such questions and say, "God can do anything. If he can create water out of nothing, he certainly can walk on it. If he can create a whale, he can create a whale that can hold a man in his stomach." (In fact, in Jules Verne's *20,000 Leagues under the Sea* the submarine, bearing a full complement of men, was mistaken for a whale by the crew of the ship it sank.) Or they say, "I don't ask questions; I have faith." Perhaps these people are lucky. As Jesus told Thomas, "Because you have seen me you have believed. Blessed are those who have believed without having seen" (John 20:29).

It is not only scientists who have such questions. And if someone has too many unanswered questions regarding the details of his faith, he eventually walks away from it. But theologians and Church people are not stupid. The same questions occur to them also, and usually many more questions, since they have studied the writings much better than most others. Although a few of them do leave the Church, most find satisfactory and intellectually honest answers to their questions. These usually involve the substitution of figurative, allegorical, or metaphorical meanings for the literal words. Obviously when Paul referred to Jesus as "our Passover lamb," he did not mean that through some wizardry Jesus was turned into a wooly, four-footed baby sheep.

Holy Writings

The Judeo-Christian Bible consists of the Old and New Testaments. The Old Testament includes the original Hebrew sacred writings: the Pentateuch, and the historical, wisdom, and prophetic books. All of them, without any exception, were written by men (or, perhaps, a woman or two) in the last millennium BC; none of them were actually written by God.

The New Testament contains the Gospels of Mark, Mathew, Luke, and John, the Acts of the Apostles, and various letters written either by Paul and Jesus' disciples or by others who used their names. There were many other gospels and writings produced in the early centuries but the Church Fathers ascribed "revealed truth" to only a few of them. One of the requirements was that only writings of Jesus' disciples could be considered revealed, that is, inspired by the Holy Spirit. The Church decreed that after the last disciple died the Holy Spirit stopped speaking through the mouth of man; God had finished talking to us.

I find this idea absurd. Jesus supposedly told his disciples that, after he left them, God would send down the Holy Comforter (the Holy Spirit) to teach them. So the Holy Fathers must have decided that by "them," Jesus had meant the twelve apostles and nobody else. Accordingly, when the twelve died, the Holy Spirit must have stopped teaching—as if Jesus had come on earth to save those twelve only! The same thing happened, incidentally, in the Hebrew religion. In the Council of Jamnia (around 90 AD) the rabbis decreed that God's last words were directed through the prophet Malachi (in 430 BC) and that God had not spoken to mankind since then. It appears that as soon as man codifies his beliefs he shuts God up in case he says something new. But I suppose that in those days, in the absence of printing presses, it was advisable to keep book revisions to a minimum.

As it turns out, it is almost certain now that none of the evangelists were Jesus' apostles or even had personally known him, and that the same holds true for most of the letter writers. The real reason why the early Christian Fathers had to limit the number of "revealed" writings is that there was no other way to control the growing beliefs of the new religion. If everyone could announce at will that he had a new revelation, then the Church's beliefs would be in continuous flux. The religion elite would have no control over it.

It would be something like the programming language UNIX at the dawn of the computer era: anybody could modify it so its rules were always changing. The result was that it proved very difficult to use UNIX in a program that everybody could access correctly. Not surprisingly, therefore, it took a long time before UNIX became standardized and widely accepted.

So, for better or worse, many early writings were relegated to the garbage heap. And under Emperor Theodosius all these "errant" writings were proscribed and actively destroyed, along with many other great pagan writings. The nascent Christian religion thus did what many other religions have done to secure their positions: it destroyed all its competitors' art and history. The most recent example of such destruction in the name of faith was the Taliban's demolition in

2001 of the two magnificent 2,000 year-old Buddha statues in Bamiya, Afghanistan.

It is true that most of the Christian writings destroyed sixteen hundred years ago consisted primarily of pure imagination and fanciful thoughts. They represented beliefs of second and third century writers about what the early teachers and martyrs would have said and done; not factual history. But it is also true that although the most revered Gospel of John forms the basis of Christianity, it does not represent real history either. One of the most important works, which barely survived destruction, is the Gospel of Thomas, a stark listing of 114 sayings of Jesus that may have even preceded the four accepted gospels.

And to help us understand the meaning of the new faith's beliefs we have the thousands upon thousands of pages written by the many wise theologians who lived during the last two millennia. Of course, not all of them are in agreement otherwise such a huge volume of writings would not have been necessary.

If all the events in Judeo-Christian history were written down generations or even centuries after they occurred, and if they were then edited time and time again, how can we justify their accuracy or even their outright veracity? A Hebrew psalmist may have rousingly extolled God's majesty, and an ancient prophet may have prefaced his prophecies by the words, "Thus said the Lord," but why should we believe that any of them spoke the actual truth? And when later scholars and theologians analyzed these words and wrote a million more words about what they mean, why should we believe that they knew the truth? Why should we assume that their ideas and stories are any more accurate than Plato's philosophizing?

Inspiration and Revelation

Ideas start with inspirations which are examined logically by the mind to arrive at conclusions. Sometimes we call such sudden inspirations "eureka moments." As the story goes, while taking his bath, the Greek mathematician Archimedes discovered the principle of buoyancy and in his great excitement ran naked out of the bathhouse into the streets of Syracuse yelling "Eureka, eureka," meaning I found. After being inspired, most ideas are expanded and amplified, sometimes resulting in unexpected conclusions.

Consider, for instance, the history behind the basic Christian Faith Doctrine, the Nicene Creed. Around 600 BC, Thales of Miletus proposed the revolutionary, for his time, idea that the world did not work in an erratic manner according to the whims of gods and demons but followed immutable logical physical rules that could be deduced. A hundred years later his follower, Heraclitus of Ephesus, named the rational principle according to which the world was created "logos." Much later Philo, a Jewish philosopher and contemporary with Jesus, expanded on the concept arguing that the logos not only represented God's rational aspect but also functioned as the head of intermediaries between God and the world. A hundred years later, John opened his salvation Gospel by preaching that in the beginning was the Logos, and the Logos was God (or *a* God, depending on how you translate the original Greek). Then, in the third century AD, Neo-Platonist Plotinus taught how the "world mind" (nous) was not created but had emanated from the One, the ground of all existence. Finally, in 325 AD, 300 bishops convened in Nicaea to declare that Jesus Christ was the Logos, the one emanated, not created, son of God. Considering what preceded it, can we consider that event a moment of inspiration or one of logical reasoning and compromise? Sometimes it is not easy to tell the difference.

True believers maintain that the holy writings were inspired by God. I agree, and would like to add that God has inspired far more than these few writings, for he is either the source of all inspiration or the source of none.

But how does God actually inspire us? In chapter 5 we discussed knowledge fields and how knowledge may be spread throughout the universe waiting to be plucked up by interested and perhaps talented persons. I pointed out that Mozart, Einstein, and others may have done exactly this while developing their symphonies or theories. Alfred Wallace arrived at his theory of evolution during a period of intermittent delirium. Mohammad, the founder of Islam, did not even know how to read, yet apparently some of the greatest poetry in the Arabic language flowed from his mouth. Where do fiction writers get their ideas from? It is true that some times they may see in the world around them something that inspires them but other times the thought may come straight out of the blue sky or, more correctly, from their own unconscious. And as discussed above, our unconscious and God may well be one and the same thing—or at least, very closely related.

Inspiration presumes communication. In order to inspire us God must communicate with us, and communication is a two-way affair. There is transmission and reception, and errors can creep in just as they do in the children's game of "telephone." One person says something but the other person understands something else. This is particularly likely when the listener already wants to hear something different from what the speaker says. We often hear what we want to hear and the rest goes by unheard. It happened when these ancient writers wrote, and it happens whenever we are interpreting their writings. But there are other factors we must also consider when we are examining the holy writings.

Allegories and Anthropomorphism

When composing a book an author has to consider what his readers know and what they are capable of understanding. It is quite obvious, for instance, that the ancient Hebrew people would have been completely incapable of understanding the physics that describe the creation of the universe; after all, how many modern Americans today are able to? So if God were to tell his people how the world and its people came to be, he would have to stay away from physics and use allegories and fairy-tale-like stories to transmit his information. We must always keep this in mind when we read the Bible. It is written in a different language, addressed to different people living in a different world. And it can only be understood in the context of the world that existed at that time.

I live in a suburb north of Chicago a little south of Half-day Road. Its name is based on the fact it was half-day's distance from the city. But that was 150 years ago when people traveled by horse-drawn buggies. Today with modern automobiles zooming on wide expressways you can make the trip in half an hour, unless, of course, it is rush hour when it will take three times that long. Many events in the Bible last for forty days. But we should not understand this to mean that the sun actually rose and set forty times while the event was taking place. In those days the number "forty" just meant a long time. The Exodus lasted forty years. This means that it lasted a long time. Creation took six days. This is a pure allegory; after all, God did not make the sun and moon to separate day from night until the fourth day.

Just as we substitute allegories for physical theories, we also use anthropomorphisms to explain philosophical concepts. You have probably seen these posters: an elderly, rather sourpuss gentleman with a goatee, wearing a suit and top hat reminiscent of the American flag, stands with his hand outstretched and his finger pointing out, with the caption reading, "Uncle Sam Wants You." Sometimes information is included about the location of the nearest Army enlistment office.

A visitor from Mars would probably think that Sam was the king of the country or some well-known military leader seeking recruits, and that calling him "uncle" just showed people's affection for him as had been the case with "Uncle Mao [Tse-tung]" during the Chinese revolution. Although few Americans know that Sam was really Samuel Wilson of Troy New York, who supplied the Federal Army with food supplies in the early 1800s, everybody knows that he represents the American nation.

And how would you represent God? The ancient Hebrews solved that problem by forbidding any reproduction of the deity, even the pronouncement of its name. But the human mind still needs to make an image of whatever it considers. So, as we saw in chapter 2, the Hebrews visualized God as something like a man and ascribed to him the highest position they could think of, that of a judge. The Christians added to this the attitude and personality of a father.

In the process the picture of God with a human shape became unconsciously etched in the human mind. And when Christianity insisted that Jesus, the God, recovered his human body before he ascended to heaven to sit at the right *hand* of his Father, their anthropomorphic qualities became even harder to reject. When Jesus, standing in front of his disciples in his sandals and robe said, "Whoever has seen me has seen the Father," what would they think that the Father looked like? Even today you will find the argument of his being *seated* at the side of his Father used to substantiate the concept of Jesus' "physical" resurrection.

Opiate of the Masses

Karl Marx called religion the opiate of the masses. He pictured in his mind the people at the bottom rungs of society facing a hopeless life of unending struggle and injustice while watching the evil, rich, and powerful reap continuous rewards. The only apparent hope for these struggling masses seemed to be a religion that promised them an after-life where God rewarded the just, punished the evil, and finally balanced the scales. And since that life would last forever the masses would get the last laugh.

The facts seem to justify Marx's claim on the appeal of religion. Looking at the nations throughout the globe we can see that religions seem to flourish wherever the living is the toughest. Christianity appears to grow fastest in strife-torn Africa and impoverished South America. Similarly, the mostly uneducated and deprived Muslim world is undergoing a religious rebirth reminiscent of its early years when it conquered and converted almost half of the known world.

In comparison, Europe has become almost completely secular, while the United States appears to be split somewhere in the middle. Here, the older generation and the passionate Evangelicals are fighting a rearguard action against the younger generation that has increasingly adopted a "Me, too" and "I want it all right now" attitude.

It is interesting to notice that at the very beginning of the Judeo-Christian story God created humanity as his greatest accomplishment: in his own image he created mankind. But it did not take long for human leaders to realize that proud people are not easily controllable. So pride was designated as the most serious of all sins, the sin that caused man's estrangement from God. God said that he created a godly man; he looked at his creation and pronounced it good. But mankind insisted that God had created a defective man; one whose very nature was base and evil. Man's only hope for eternal salvation depended on strictly following the rules set forth by God's representatives on earth, the priests.

As society progressed the priests ceded some of their power to the kings. Now it was the kings who represented God on earth; one had to follow his king's orders as if they were God's. From the Egyptian pharaohs to Louis XV this concept of the divine right of kings lasted for millennia. Even Paul agreed with it. And today the head of the Roman Catholic Church, the pope, is considered to be God's direct representative on earth. When he speaks ex-cathedra he cannot be wrong. So it appears that religion is not only the opiate of the masses but also the tool of its leaders.

After-Life Ideas

Of course not all religions agree with what the next life is like. The Hindus, for instance, believe in the concept of reincarnation, according to which the soul keeps recycling through various existences on earth until it attains perfection. But the lack of many human specimens approaching perfection may indicate that humanity may well destroy its world before it reaches that goal. I will grant you, however, that the prospect of returning to earth as a cockroach would pose a strong deterrent to my pursuing a life of egotism and plunder.

The spread of Islam, especially during its early years, was greatly helped by the belief that those who die killing the infidel are guaranteed a place in heaven surrounded by seventy-two virgins. Of course, in order for this to continue throughout eternity it is obvious that these virgins will have to retain their virginal state, something that apparently is not widely appreciated by the militant faithful.

Christianity, with which most of us are better acquainted, makes a clear separation between heaven, where the good guys go, and hell, where the bad ones are sent. These places are not described in detail. But hell seems to be a place of fire, like Gehenna, where the ancient Jerusalemites used to burn their garbage, from which rise the shrieks of the eternally tortured. The only descriptions of heaven are found in Revelation, where the faithful are portrayed standing in circles around God's throne dressed in white robes and singing "Holy, holy" forever. The difference between the two places seems to be only one of degree unless you happen to be an unwavering gospel singer.

The Religion Business

During the three centuries that followed the death of Jesus thousands of Christians died horribly in the persecutions ordered by the Roman emperors. The last and most widespread of these was in 303-305 AD during the reign of Emperor Diocletian. All this changed, however, when Constantine became emperor, first of the Eastern and then of the combined Roman Empire. In quick order, freedom of religion was ordered, Christianity was proclaimed the official religion of the empire, and finally, all pagan faiths were outlawed and Judaism oppressed. Christianity suddenly found itself the recipient of huge Treasury largesse and inheritor of many pagan edifices and temples, those, at least, that were not utterly destroyed by the fury that the new Christian emperors unleashed toward pagan and Hellenistic cultures.

Constantine, however, was not a philosopher or theologian searching for the true God but an emperor attempting to govern a sprawling empire that encompassed a large number of ethnic nationalities and racial cultures. He envisioned a single religion as the glue that would help pull together this wide assortment of peoples and ideas. And being a soldier, he did what every good soldier knows how to do. He set out to destroy all opposition, starting from the numerous Christian sects, the Donatists and the Gnostics, and culminating with the pagans. By the time the Theodosian Code was published in 438 AD, the practice of pagan worship and other heresies were punishable by death, and Jews had lost all their rights.

Christianity changed from a religion that followed Jesus' teachings to a government department and, under the Roman papacy, into a sovereign nation itself. Under the pretext of protecting or spreading Christianity the papacy dispatched an army of Crusaders to the Holy Land killing the infidels "until their blood came to the knees of the horses." The Church sent monks and priests to accompany Columbus and the Conquistadors to save the souls of the savages even if it required burning them alive. In 1555 pope Paul IV restricted Jews to a wall-enclosed ghetto in a four-block flood-prone area of Rome, an edict that was not abolished until the newly formed Kingdom of Italy conquered Rome in 1870. It took another eighteen years before the wall was torn down.

In recent years religion has been widely used by many nations to justify the occupation of their neighbors' land or removal of undesirables from their own area. It has even acquired its own name; it is now called "ethnic cleansing." In the 1940s Germany's leader, Adolph Hitler, ordered the murder of seven million Jews, Gypsies, Slavs, and other undesirables. In the 1980s the Christian Serbs massacred thousands of Muslim Kosovars. For the last ten years the Muslim Sudanese in the north have been trying to eliminate the Christian Arab blacks in the south, in order to take over their land. And, finally, for the last half-century the modern Jews and Palestinians have been killing each other in a battle for possession of the Holy Land.

And what did God do after all this? I imagine him looking down at his creation, hiding his face behind a cloud, and pronouncing sadly, "It is NOT good." Let us now turn our attention from religion to God.

PEANUTS

12/9/05
YOU'RE MINE! I HAVE MADE YOU WITH MY OWN HANDS!

AND, LEST YOU FORGET, AS I CREATED YOU, I ALSO CAN DESTROY YOU!!
© 1969 United Feature Syndicate, Inc.

www.snoopy.com

I'M SORRY... THAT WAS A STUPID THING TO SAY...
SCHULZ

CHAPTER 9

GOD, LOVE, AND EVIL

"I brought you into this world, and I swear I'm going to take you right out of it this instant if you don't stop!" my neighbor would yell at her kids when they had tested her patience a little too far. My neighbors were of Scandinavian descent; they were giants—a little gruff, perhaps, but kind, physical giants. And despite all the threats, their children survived and grew up to be giants also. But, of course, nobody really believed all that yelling.

But what sense can we make of the moody and ever-changing God of the Bible? This God alternates from a loving parent one minute, granting his child's every need before it is even voiced, to an enraged monarch who throws an inappropriately dressed guest out into the darkness where there is always wailing and gnashing of teeth (Matthew 22:13). Today's society would diagnose such a person as schizophrenic or bipolar and immediately prescribe medication.

In this short chapter we will look at the Judeo-Christian God and the dual personalities that Christianity attributes to him. We will then discuss why a good and powerful God created so much evil in this world or, at least, permits it to exist.

Love

What is love? Here is my definition: it is a very strong feeling of like or desire, of affection or attraction towards something or somebody DESPITE its consequences and WITHOUT the need for any logical justification. Love can be good, bad, or indifferent. To love knowledge is good; to love danger is, to say the least, dangerous.

A parent's love for his offspring is an innate drive required for the biological survival of a species and can be found throughout much of the animal kingdom. This gives special importance to Jesus' description of God as our heavenly Father. If he is our father God must love us even if we are not worthy of it. The situation is different in the Old Testament, where God generally just shows mercy instead of love (although some translations do substitute the word "love"). In two or three instances the Old testament God is presented as loving the righteous, but it is easy to love the righteous; loving the unworthy is the true expression of love.

In John's Gospel, Jesus ordered his disciples to love one another as he had loved them. In the other gospels he preached that we should love God with all our heart and our neighbors as ourselves. And Jesus loved everybody, although he did berate many. Even while hanging from the cross he asked God to forgive his killers. So clearly love is the most important concept that jumps out at us from the New Testament. But I should specify that it is not just any kind of love, not love for money or power, for example, but love for people, love for God's creation.

Even if we were to ignore God, we cannot deny that love for God's creation has a remarkable effect on the human soul; it transforms one into a kinder, happier, healthier, better person. Even loving an animal makes a difference. It has been scientifically proven that pets lower their owner's blood pressure, add to the life expectancy of older people, and give pleasure to those confined in a nursing home. And as my daughter who works at an animal hospital says, it is often far easier to love a pet than its owner.

Pets, in fact, reveal the need humans have for love. Why else would someone adopt something that he has to feed, clean up after, and take to the vet; something that restricts his own freedom to come and go as he pleases, something that definitely costs money? What does a pet owner receive for his efforts? The only conceivable answer is love. Pets love you, but even more important they offer you the opportunity to love them. I tell my children that I have kids so I don't need pets; but they contend that my kids have grown up and don't count, and so they keep filling my home, and theirs, with dogs and cats. At the very moment I was writing this, in fact, one of these lovable felines they have bestowed upon me was throwing up on my carpet.

As we saw in chapter 2, the heads of some of the largest Christian denominations in the world summarized their beliefs with the statement that "God is love." But if God is love, why does he allow so much evil to exist in the world? Why does he, in fact, apparently create it? If God is love, why does he consign people to eternal damnation? Let's look at these questions one at a time.

The Problem of Evil

My dictionary defines the word "theodicy" as the defense of God's goodness and omnipotence in view of the existence of evil in the world. Why would a God who is good and who can do anything, allow evil to exist? Why does he not stop it, eradicate it completely? It is a problem that has baffled theologians throughout the ages. "God has his reasons," or "God knows what is best for us," are some of the lame justifications that are offered to explain why bad things happen.

When the fox chases the rabbit, whose side are you on? If you say the rabbit, the fox starves; if you select the fox, the rabbit dies. Rain may be good for the farmer but bad for the builder who is pouring concrete. It appears that so much of the evil in the world is relative; it depends on where you stand when you are looking at it.

What about the earthquake that kills thousands? Where is the good in that? Earthquakes are the result of the basic physical processes that form continents and mountains, the solid ground on which we live. "But if God is omnipotent," you will say, "he could do all this without earthquakes." The obvious answer to this is that God is not omnipotent. Even the ancient Hebrews did not think he was omnipotent; powerful, yes, but not omnipotent.

Furthermore, much of the evil that befalls us is the result of our ignorance or our unwillingness to act in accordance with what we know is right. We smoke, and we die of cancer. We drink, and we get cirrhosis of the liver. We take part in unprotected sex, and we end up with AIDS or other sexual diseases. We drive drunk, and we kill or maim ourselves or others. The pregnant mother-to-be takes the brand-new drug thalidomide to cure her headache, and her child is born without arms. We build houses on a covered-up toxic waste disposal site called Love Canal, and the inhabitants suffer cancer and a host of other diseases. A bunch of fanatics fly two airplanes into the World Trade Center and kill three thousand people. No matter where you look, whatever bad or good happens to us in our life is either the result of natural forces or human acts. We cannot in good conscience blame God for all these events. Yet we do.

Early on August 27, 2006, while it was still dark, Captain Jeffrey Clay and his co-pilot James Polehinke boarded their Comair flight 5191 regional jet at Blue Grass Airport in Lexington, Kentucky, and prepared to take off. Actually it was the second plane they boarded, since they mistakenly first entered the wrong one. Captain Clay then proceeded to taxi to the incorrect runway, one that was half as long as necessary, and turned the controls over to his co-pilot who attempted the take-off despite noticing that the runway lights were off. The plane crashed at the end of the short runway, killing everybody on board except the co-pilot. The tower operator might have prevented the disaster but he had been working alone, in contravention to FAA rules, and had turned around to do some paperwork.

One of the first things Polehinke said when he woke up in his hospital bed was, “Why did God do this to me?” “It was not God, it was an accident,” answered his mother. But notice how our first reaction is to blame God for whatever bad things happen to us. In reality, of course, it was all a result of human errors: first the pilots taxied to the wrong runway, then they ignored the darkened lights, and finally the controller did not notice the mistake because he was working alone against the rules. If anything, God had tried to send them a "Be alert" message when they first boarded the wrong plane.

What about those who believe that there exists an evil power in the world, Satan, or other evil spirits that actively try to influence us to cause evil? Shouldn't God do something about it? Well, if Satan and evil spirits exist then they are a part of the universe, just like mosquitoes and rattlesnakes. Furthermore, if spirits are part of the life cycle we should expect to encounter both good spirits and bad spirits. Regarding mosquitoes and snakes, we must admit that evolution results in the development of all sorts of creatures, both beneficial and detrimental to humans.

There cannot be good without evil, light without dark, yin without yang. Some things are not recognizable without their opposites. How can you recognize happiness unless you have experienced unhappiness? It might be possible, perhaps, to design a world in which every species magically controlled its population without the need of a predator but, unfortunately, this is not such a world. It might be possible, perhaps, to design animals that never act stupidly or do evil, but they would not be human.

The universe is an incredible self-balancing entity that operates by following certain basic physical rules. And a balancing act requires that for every action there is an equal reaction. The result is a self-sustaining universe, one that does not require continuous external control. It is like a plane on autopilot: it keeps going in the proper direction, automatically adjusting for updrafts and wind changes. But turn off the autopilot, and then the continuous attention of the pilot will be required. After God created the universe, if he did, he turned on his autopilot; he did not settle down to an eternity of performing minor tunings and adjustments. God does not select the strength of a hurricane any more that the president of General Motors decides the proper torque value for tightening the lug nuts on the automobile wheels of a particular car model.

But how about sending people to hell? How can one justify that a loving God created mankind while fully knowing that he would send much of it to eternal damnation? That is the subject of our next chapter.

BIZARRO

Try to keep in mind this is an allegory
& you're actually off evolving from
apes somewhere right now.
© DAN PIRARO
BIZARRO.COM
9-29-03

CHAPTER 10

SIN AND PUNISHMENT

The defining point of humanity, according to the Judeo-Christian religion, occurred very soon after its creation when the first couple sinned by breaking God's command and ate the forbidden apple. In the Old Testament sin is defined as man's disobedience of God's commands. The result is a sinful mankind living in a broken world. And, according to Christian religion, humanity's redemption was accomplished only when God became incarnated as the human Jesus and died on the cross.

But most Christians today understand that the Adam and Eve story is only an allegory, a fable attempting to explain why a perfect God appears to have created an imperfect universe. Furthermore, the history of our planet does not indicate that Creation ever was, or could have been, in a state of perfection from which it fell at some point. And just as history denies the possibility of original sin, science questions the notion of everyday conscious sin by arguing that human free will does not exist. So, God punishing me in the next life for the sins I committed in this one makes no more sense than if I were to spank my dog for killing the bunny that carelessly crossed his path. In fact it makes less sense, because it is possible that through proper discipline I may be able to train my dog to leave bunnies alone, whereas the idea that we will be punished to improve us does not appear anywhere in the Bible.

In the New Testament, however, the Greek word that is translated as SIN (using caps to distinguish it from the theological sin discussed above) means not to disobey God's command but to miss hitting the mark on a target, as in archery; something entirely different. According to this definition, SIN is not disobedience but lack of perfection.

And although practice can improve one's performance, none of us can attain our theoretical perfection because none of us are physically or mentally perfect. We all suffer from numerous defects that originated in the past and over which we currently have no control, such as defective genes, prenatal problems, and improper upbringing. Original and everyday SINS, therefore, are not infractions for which we should be punished, but infections from which we should get cured. Even so we do not escape suffering for our SINS. God may be forgiving, but infections take their toll, even if they eventually get cured.

Theological Sin

We are told that Jesus came to bring the Good News. And the good news is that God is with us and that we will have everlasting life. Unless, of course, you are an unforgiven sinner, in which case you end up in eternal hell. According to religious nomenclature, sin means to transgress God's laws and, according to Christianity, almost everybody is a sinner. And when Jesus added the stipulation that sinful thoughts are as bad as actual sinful deeds, even the most resolutely good people were shut out of paradise. So it is not surprising that when Jesus' disciples asked him who could be saved under such stringent conditions he answered: "With men this is impossible, but with God all things are possible" (Mat. 19:26).

But just in case there were one or two really saintly people who neither did nor thought evil, Paul and the Roman Church added their concept of "original sin": In the beginning, at the creation of the world, the first human couple sinned by disobeying God, and since then their sin has been transmitted undiminished down to all subsequent generations. Thus we are all sinners from the minute we are born, no matter how piously we live. It appears that heaven may be a very empty place indeed. Fortunately, according to Christian beliefs, God sent his own son to earth in the human form of Jesus, who, by dying on the cross, redeemed mankind (or at least the part that believes in him) from the result of the original sin.

Two questions arise: what was the original sin, and how did Jesus' death on the cross save mankind, or at least believers, from its results? The answers, however, do not belong in this book. I discussed the ideas of the early Church in *Christianity without Fairy Tales*, and the grown Christian Church has produced volumes of writings on the subject; for a quick overview, just Google the term "original sin." Let me prepare you, however: the explanations are not any clearer than Bohm's ideas about implicate fields.

I will limit myself, therefore, to a simple question: who were these ancestors of ours who performed this sin, whatever it may have been? Scientists tell us that humans originally evolved in Africa and then between 50,000 and 25,000 BC they migrated across Europe and Asia. The early ones learned how to use fire and complex tools, and they probably had some kind of language. Are we to assume that one of these people somehow sinned against God by breaking his orders? And that God is still punishing us for that? And that the only way he could find to forgive us was to send his only son to die on the cross? Simple logic, I believe, requires that we dispense with this concept.

Although the story of the original sin appears at the very beginning of the Jewish Bible, the ancient Hebrews did not pay too much attention to it. The original sin, however, is the cornerstone of Paul's Christianity. Christ redeemed us from its consequences either by sacrificing himself for the atonement of our sins, or by conquering Satan who had gained power over humans after the original couple's sin. The first argument was directed to the Jews, the second to the Gentiles.

Volumes have been written on this subject, but they really don't concern us in this book. After all, Christ is supposed to be the divine son of the Hebrew God Yahweh who, as I have argued, is an anthropomorphic construct of our forefathers and whose existence and adventures belong to the realm of myth and religion, not science. Nevertheless, the existence of sin is one more area of agreement between science and religion, provided we redefine the term in non-theistic terms.

Natural SIN

The Greek word that is used for "SIN" in the Bible is "hamartia." Without any direct religious connotations it means to miss the mark, as in archery. To differentiate *hamartia* from the religious sin we discussed above, we will capitalize the entire word SIN. So in this book, when the term is applied to humanity, SIN refers to something that causes us to miss our growth potential. Accordingly, original SIN is something that prevents all of mankind from attaining its full potential; from becoming all it can be. Although religion cannot find a historical, non-mythical justification for such a concept, science has come to its aid. The discovery of genes and DNA, along with the realization that we all possess some defective copies of them, has made it abundantly clear that none of us are physically capable of being perfect. We can make this idea clearer by expanding the definition of SIN to include not only our own actions that lack perfection but also the causes that inhibit us from acting perfectly. According to such an expanded definition, defective DNA can be considered to be a SIN. Here is another case where science substantiates, both theoretically and experimentally, an allegory found in the Bible.

We do indeed suffer from the results of original SINS; both those that have occurred in our ancestors' life and those in our own past. In addition to defective DNA inherited from our ancestors, a pregnant mother's poor diet or drug habits, and the manner in which we were raised, can and do affect our growth potential. These are only a few of the scientifically identified original SINS that prevent us from reaching our full potential. We will look at this subject again in the chapter 11 when we discuss the human growth cycle.

Predestination and Free Will

I argued above that theological original sin does not exist and that natural original SIN is beyond our control since it happened in the past. But what about current sins and SINS? What about our everyday acts that are against God's commands or provoke undesirable reactions from nature? My neighbor may not own a camel for me to covet but his Lexus appears extremely desirable. And although the Ten Commandments do not include "Thou shall not get drunk," I do know that if I imbibe a little too freely my good judgment will fail and I may commit errors for which I will be sorry later. Should I not be punished for these transgressions? Depending on many factors I might or might not get punished here on earth; we already discussed that unfairness reigns in this world. But what about the hereafter: shouldn't God punish me?

From the theological point of view, I should be punished for my transgressions if I did them knowingly and freely. But for God to punish me, two things must hold true: I must know that an action is wrong, and I must be free to decide how to act. Examining the first point, whether we innately know good from evil (I believe that we don't), will get us into a long and inconclusive argument, so I will pass this over and concentrate instead on the second: am I free to choose between two alternatives? Do I have free will?

The matter of free will arose early in theological history. It was argued that because God did not want to be adored by mindless creatures he bestowed free will to humans so that they could decide what they wanted to do. They could love him and follow his laws or go their own way and be damned. I will ignore the little detail about how he apparently granted them free will before they ate the fruit from the tree of knowledge, before they had learned how to differentiate between good and evil, an argument suggesting that the mythical pair sinned before it even knew what sin was.

The important point here is that at some point during his development man was either given or developed the capability for logical reasoning; something that allows him to reach decisions by examining the information stored in his brain and then rationally evaluating the available courses of action according to their perceived merits. This is something computers do really well these days. And since computers are faster than human brains they always beat humans at the ultimate logic game, chess.

Logical reasoning involves evaluation of past knowledge, knowledge that was gained before the moment of decision. But at any one instant in our life we are not in control of what we know. All our knowledge originated in the past, and we have to use this past knowledge to make logical decisions in the present. Logic is like one of those old-fashioned scales, the one that the blindfolded statue of Justice in Washington holds in her hand. You put all the pros on one tray, all the cons on the other, and the side that sinks indicates which one prevails. But what we place on our decision-making trays are the facts that we have learned in our past, and since we cannot change our past we have no control of how the balance tilts. Our decision is preordained, unless the balance is unbalanced.

There are defective balances, and there are defective minds. But that is another thing over which we have no control at the moment of decision. We have to use the balance we have, the mind we have. (In fact, scientists tell us that the part of the brain that is responsible for controlling impulses and making moral judgments does not even mature until our twenties.) In any case, whatever problem exists with our minds has also happened in the past and is beyond our control now. So, whether healthy or not, a logical person is restricted in his ability to decide freely. If you know everything about me, you should be able to predict all my actions and decisions.

But many decisions bypass logic completely. Simple logic, for instance, would counsel that it is stupid to give money to the poor since not only it does not yield any tangible benefit but it also reduces the funds available for fulfilling our own egotistical needs. Admittedly, making a charitable contribution apparently activates the pleasure centers in our brain, but why? So people contribute to the poor; some throughout their lives, and some at the end of their lives when they realize, perhaps, that their money will do them no good where they are going. Among these last are those few people we occasionally hear about who, though working in modest occupations, live very frugal lives accumulating substantial amounts of money that, upon their death, they bequeath to their favorite projects. Analyzing their actions would be the subject of an interesting debate but outside the scope of our work.

Man is an emotional being; one who laughs and cries, who hopes when logically there is no hope left, who occasionally dies to protect his fellow beings. As Mr. Spock and Captain Kirk of the Starship *Enterprise* clearly showed, although emotions are not logical they obviously play a part in the decisions that humans make. But are we in control of them?

Scientists tell us that emotions reside in the paleo-mammalian brain, the second of the three brains that nature developed, and in the limbic system, its neural extensions throughout the body. And both of these are affected by the chemical balances in our brain and the rest of our body. Obviously we have no conscious control over any of them, although at times we can consciously modify our external responses. If I get in a heated discussion, for instance, I may not be able to control my rising blood pressure but, if I remember to make a conscious effort, sometimes I can keep my voice level down.

It is generally accepted that most of the factors affecting our emotional responses to outside stimuli lie hidden in our subconscious (or unconscious). This is why psychiatrists are so interested in those life events that elicit seemingly disproportional reactions; because they point to the existence of important factors that affect our judgment but of which we may be completely unaware. Furthermore, as we saw in chapter 7, it is possible that we reach most of our decisions entirely in our unconscious without any conscious evaluation of them. Obviously, in that case there exists no conscious freedom of choice.

What would constitute freedom of choice, if it existed? Let me propose that it would be our capability to react in contravention of all laws, both natural and social. Otherwise we would apply these laws to determine how we should respond to any situation we encounter, just as we actually do when we solve other physical problems in the universe. But our earlier discussion concluded that both our conscious reasoning and our emotional reactions are based on historical events and biological factors over which we currently have no power. If the past controls our present, and we obviously cannot change the past, then we have no control of our present, either. This is the logical argument. The scientific argument was presented back in chapter 7, where it was claimed that we react to our environment before we have an opportunity to reach a conscious decision about what to do.

As Einstein supposedly said, man may be able to do what he wants but he is not able to consciously decide what he wants. It appears that we are just puppets pretending that we are in charge of the script of life when in reality every one of our actions is controlled by the puppet-master's hidden strings. If this statement sounds familiar, look back to the discussion on synchronicity in chapter 1.

Punishment

Final judgment of the soul resulting in its eternal punishment or reward is one of the most basic concepts in Christian theology. "When the Son of man shall come in his glory...he will set the sheep on his right hand and the goats on his left.... He will say to those on his right hand, 'Come ye blessed inherit the kingdom prepared for you'...and he will say to the ones on his left, 'Depart from me ye cursed into everlasting fire....'" (Mat 25:31-46). If we are not responsible for our actions what would be God's justification for punishing us for our misdeeds?

Why, indeed, do we punish people? One reason is to get even: he hit me, I hit him back. Another is to chastise somebody for acting badly: my child lost his temper and smashed the vase, so I reprimanded him. Another is to teach a lesson: he wrote all over the wall with his crayons, so I had him wash all the walls in the room.

Christianity has also proposed a completely different mechanism affecting punishment: we are all sinners and thus we should all be punished, but God arbitrarily selects some to whom he shows mercy. This is a Calvinist belief and appears to claim that our actions are irrelevant, that our fate has been predestined and we have no control over it. Both Paul and John offer instances of this (Rom: 9-15, John: 6-65). But this turns God into a capricious being that, without any apparent reason, saves some while damning others. Since the early days of Christianity countless theologians have discussed this apparent inference without reaching a satisfactory explanation.

I don't think that God would punish us to get even. After all, Jesus said turn the other cheek. Punishing us for acting badly does not make much sense either if we have no control over our actions. That leaves only one acceptable reason for God to punish us, to teach us to become better. And that means that there can be no eternal and everlasting punishment, no matter what your Bible or Church says. Wherever the Bible records this, it is false; if Jesus was quoted saying something like it, either he was quoted wrongly or he was wrong. One of the basic changes that Christianity must introduce in its doctrine, if it expects to attract thinking people, is the elimination of the concept of eternal hell and punishment for one's bad actions during his life. As offensive as it may appear to many, even Genghis Khan's and Adolph Hitler's souls will eventually be rehabilitated and will escape eternal torment.

Escaping punishment for our actions, however, does not mean that we also escape suffering. I am nailing two boards together, my attention slips and I hammer my thumb instead of the nail. Nobody punished me for my inattention, but it still hurts. As we will see in the next chapter, even if God does not punish us for our misdeeds we may still suffer because of them.

LAUGH PARADE

"AGNES, THAT'S NOT WHAT I MEANT WHEN I SAID, 'GET A LIFE!'"

CHAPTER 11

LIFE CYCLES

"What the caterpillar calls the end of the world the rest of the world calls butterfly."

—Richard Bach

There are a few species in the world, that live through two completely distinct forms. Tadpoles turn into frogs and caterpillars into butterflies. The latter's metamorphosis is far more dramatic. I am proposing here that an even more extraordinary transformation takes place during death when our spiritual (energy) soul is set free from our physical body. But just as the original condition of the physical body depends on the conditions it encountered while in the womb, so also the original quality of the soul depends on how well it grew during its years on earth.

Being without our physical body will probably be the greatest change we experience in the next world.

Physical bodies have many disadvantages but the greatest one, perhaps, is that they act as a wall keeping us away from each other. What happens when you take down a wall or a barrier? Better communication, more closeness. What we value the most in this life is being close to our loved ones; so in the afterlife the lack of physical barriers should permit our energy spirits to snuggle close together, perhaps even to merge with each other.

Fetus

And now the time has come to talk about the birds, the bees, and the butterflies. A human life starts its journey when its father's spermatozoon encounters its mother's egg, combines with it, and begins its growth and subdivision process. Eventually, if everything goes well, the growing fetus starts acquiring a human likeness and within nine months it physically grows into a finished, though tiny, human being complete with fingernails and hair fuzz. Somewhere during this period the future baby even acquires a brain and the ability to use it in a rudimentary fashion. But scientists are not sure when exactly the brain acquires consciousness or, better yet, awareness. Although the fetus is always physically affected by metabolic changes in its mother's body, during the last months it can probably also hear sounds and sense its physical environment. Some parents believe that playing Mozart to the fetus during this stage increases its intelligence.

But as with many other such ideas this is more commonly found among first-time parents.

So when does the fetus become a human? The answer to this question has become crucial in the abortion debate and, of course, it is really based on the definition of human life. The pro-life groups maintain either that anything that can grow into a human is human life, or that God-given souls are attached to the egg at the instant it is penetrated by a spermatozoon. I will let philosophers analyze the statement that something already is what it has the possibility of becoming. I would rather concentrate on the timing of when the body acquires the soul.

In chapter 7, I argued that a soul contains memory and, perhaps, some personality characteristics. So by that definition the fetus does not have a soul until it develops a brain and memory. But memory alone does not make a fetus human. My dogs and cats also have memories, but nobody will confuse them with humans. The converse, however, is true. If animals have memories, then they also have souls. In fact, my definition seems to indicate that a one-year-old dog's soul might be more developed than the soul of a week-old baby. We will return to this point a little later.

I have had many arguments with Christian believers who insist that the soul that survives the death of the physical body does not have any memories of its earthly life, although it somehow contains the "essence" of the individual; they are unable, however, to define what this "essence" is. Unfortunately, postulating the existence of some unknown, indefinable property limits all further discussion to general inanities. If we can't even guess what something might be, how can we discuss it? In any case, I defined what I mean by soul at the outset of chapter 7.

Scientists tell us that the life of the fetus is extraordinarily stress-free. All its physical needs are automatically taken care of, its environment always remains at a perfect temperature, food is delivered on schedule, and it does not have to take any exams or balance checkbooks. Even its crowded world may not be as much of a drawback as we think. Consider that mental patients who try to completely withdraw from the world often assume the fetal position. The fetus's happy existence, however, ends with birth: a trip down the birth canal, which must be one of the most stressful experiences that humans ever experience. Fortunately, we cannot remember it.

Human

The change from the protected womb to the noisy, bright, cold environment of the outside world must be quite a shock to the infant. Yet it immediately starts learning with its tiny brain growing at a rapid rate while millions of neurons make new connections to record and accommodate the environmental stimuli cascading upon it. For the neurons it is a time of "use it or lose it"; those that do nothing are discarded as superfluous.

Although the brain has now forgotten its months in the womb, the body has not. As we saw in the last chapter, it is not the sins of the fathers that are transmitted to the child, as the Bible says, but those of the mother's. Did she eat properly, take her vitamins, watch her health, or did she neglect taking good care of herself and smoked, drank, or even took drugs? All these things affect not only the body but, more importantly, the developing brain of the infant. Babies born with drug withdrawal or HIV symptoms are only two immediately noticeable examples of how a mother's actions affect her baby's welfare. Much of the baby's future life depends on things that happened while it was in the womb, things that were beyond its control.

But as was the case with the fetus, the quickly maturing infant has very little control of its environment. What it is fed, how it is treated, whether it is loved, whether it is neglected, how it is punished, all these things affect both its body and mind. Within a few years they will be forgotten, yet they will be influencing the grown person's actions and thoughts forever. For those still looking for the source of original sin, look here also. We don't need to create imaginary, prehistoric ancestors who sinned; our own parents and caregivers have provided us with the sturdy or rickety foundation on which the rest of our lives are built.

I don't need to say much about this life. We are all in it, and we all have our own opinions about it. Some think it is wonderful; others think it is a drag. Some feel they should make a positive contribution to the world while they are here; others think that the world owes them a lifetime of leisure and entertainment. Some try to lift up their fellow humans; others step on as many as they can in their effort to climb higher. But no matter how one lives it, all lives have one thing in common: they all end. And that leads us to the greatest mystery of them all.

What Is Next?

I have already discussed my beliefs regarding the existence of an afterlife. But what kind of afterlife it is, no one knows; I am certain, however, that when our time comes we will all find out. Perhaps the greatest adventure of our life is waiting at its end; an end that most of us fear because it is natural for people to fear the unknown. An end that comes too soon for many people and, perhaps, too late for others; many people who have lived full, busy lives find it extremely difficult to adjust to the arrival of physical and mental deterioration during their last years.

My mother was an avid reader, but towards the end of her life she only needed one book: "By the time I reach the end I have forgotten the beginning," she used to say. But when she finally became unable to concentrate on reading even that one book, some time after she had lost interest in her soap operas, boredom became overbearing. Nevertheless, she had definite expectations of what was waiting for her in the next world. It would be a world where one could do whatever one had always wanted to do, where mental and physical disabilities disappeared, a place without pain or sorrow. "When I wake up in the morning and nothing hurts, then I'll know I'm dead," she used to say. She had decided that she was going to take up ice skating then, something she had always wanted to do but never had the opportunity.

It is unfortunate that for most persons the entry to the next world comes only after days of pain and suffering in this one. Sadly, society permits us to be infinitely kinder to our aged and infirm pets than to our aged and infirm parents. Perhaps if people ever realize that the end of our earthly life represents only the beginning of our next life, maybe they will stop being so intent in keeping us alive at any cost even after most of our organs have started shutting down.

So according to what we discussed in chapter 7, once the mind ceases to exhibit signs of electrical activity the body dies and the soul is free. And this soul must be capable of fulfilling Descartes's logic, "I think, therefore I am." In addition, we decided that in order for the soul to exist it must be part of some kind of electromagnetic field, perhaps of the same nature as the universe. If, for instance, the basic structure of the universe consists of infinitely small vibrating

NON SEQUITUR

strings then the soul can be assumed to consist of them also. It is thus a part of the universe. And if God is the result of the interconnections between these strings, then the soul must also be a part of God.

Two thousand years ago the Gnostics visualized the divine sparks of the liberated souls fending off the satanic principalities on their way to reach and merge with God. In the Gnostic Gospel of Thomas (no. 50) Jesus advises his disciples how they should respond when they are stopped and questioned by the evil powers during their ascent: “If they say to you, ‘Where did you come from?’ say to them, ‘We come from the light, the place where the light came into being on its own accord and established itself and became manifest through its image.’ If they say to you, ‘Is it you?’ say to them, ‘We are its children, and we are the elect of the living father.’”

But notice that if according to our assumptions all matter and hence also our physical body structure consists of energy, then even in our current form we are already a part of God; except that the physical body gets in the way. It is one thing to walk on the beach barefoot in your swimsuit, and another to do it in a spacesuit; the bulky suit gets in the way. This would be even more noticeable if you were trying to hold hands with your sweetheart. And here may lie hidden the greatest advantage of our next life: better, fuller, more intimate communication with those we love. I believe that just as related particles in the electromagnetic fields can communicate with each other, so can souls also. "When you make the two one, and when you make the inside like the outside and the outside like the inside...then will you enter the Kingdom" (Gospel of Thomas, no. 22).

So what about my poor mother's plans to learn ice skating? I can't imagine disembodied souls skating. But I can imagine a complete and intimate sharing of the pleasure of skating and other such activities between those souls that had done them and those who would like to do them. And this leads us to the next possibility, that of two or more souls becoming one. Can souls merge together to become super-souls, replacing their individual distinctiveness with a collective self? Is this why people generally see ghosts of the recently dead and not of those who died long ago? Is this why it is unlikely that Jesus will ever return, because he does not exist as an individual entity anymore but as part of God? Is Christianity right after all, that even though Jesus walked the earth as a man he is now God?

But in our discussion on ghosts in chapter 6, I said that some souls may not leave the physical realm when their time comes. They may decide to stick around and scare or fascinate their still earthbound fellow-beings. Suppose that my mother's soul did not search for the soul of a dead skater with whom to exchange experiences but instead hung around the skating arena feeding off the emotions of the young skaters. Now we are coming close to what is called possession: instances where a soul remains near the physical realm and tries to experience physical cravings directly by becoming attached to a living being.

Just as our life as a fetus affected our earthly existence, so our earthly life may affect how easily we adapt to our spiritual existence. It is not only physical barriers that keep people apart, but mental barriers also. We can prepare for the next world, therefore, by starting to lower our mental barriers and getting closer to people now. And the best way to do this is to open up to one another, love one another. Living a loving, helpful life as adults is similar to doing our homework as children. Just as knowledge we acquired as children helped us when we grew up, so a loving and helpful life as an adult will help us in our spirit life. Love not only changes this world but prepares us for the next one.

Final Judgment

Civil laws presume the existence of a court system that punishes the miscreant; the concept of theological sin assumes that the offender will be eventually judged and punished. Scripture is full of admonitions to both believers and nonbelievers alike. Yet, as we discussed in the previous chapter, the punishments threatened in the Bible far exceed any standards of measured response. Surely no earthly sin merits eternal punishment. Modern theologians have responded by postulating that it is not God who punishes the guilty, but it is the guilty who punish themselves by staying away from God.

I have argued in this book against the existence of free will, willful sinners, and theological sin. But we have seen that SIN does exist, provided that we define it as our parents' actions or other environmental factors that have reduced our ability to perform fully in life. Suffering for offenses beyond our control seems unfair, but it is a fact of life. So although no divine court waits for us in the afterlife, everybody may not fare equally well. Just as our human lives suffer from deficiencies that existed during the time we spent in the fetus, so our future lives may be affected by events that occurred in our earthly lives.

In this book I have set forth two postulates:

1. The soul contains the memories and some parts of our personality.

2. The main discernible advantage of the afterlife is sharing and being close to others.

We can conclude from these that the person who tried in his life to relate with and help his fellow beings will find it much easier to adjust and grow in the next life than the egotistical "I want it all and the heck with you" person. Just as our life in the womb prepared us for our life on earth, so our life on earth prepares us for our life in the hereafter. Although there may not be such a place as hell, some souls may find it much harder to adjust to the transformation and grow. Fortunately they will be afforded an infinite amount of time to do it.

Interestingly, many people who had near-death experiences described seeing their entire life passing before their eyes and becoming conscious of the harm they had done to others; but none reported the presence of a judge. It is not that we are the judges of our past actions as modern theologians may tell us, but that we are the results of our past actions; they have molded us into what we are. Perhaps this is unfair but it seems that life is unfair, at least in the manner in which we usually understand that word.

And what happens to the souls of those who die very young? If our current life is a preparation for the next one, as I maintain, it would be like moving someone from kindergarten directly into college. But we can assume that this "hereafter college" offers remedial classes, perhaps taught by more advanced souls. And where do animal souls fit in? Are their souls limited to the amount of growth they can attain? Frankly, I have no idea. But if all souls eventually become one, perhaps we can accept Paul's observation that even though all the parts in a body are not equal they are all necessary (1 Cor. 12). Even on earth dogs and dolphins often exhibit an uncanny ability to help and empathize with the physically and mentally impaired. Cats, birds, even mice enrich the lives of many. If they all belong to this world I am sure that they all belong to the next one also.

I can't prove any of this, of course, but it all sounds reasonable to me.

The Way of the Monarch Butterfly

It all starts when the mother butterfly attaches her eggs to the underside of milkweed leaves with a kind of quick-drying glue that she secretes. Then, after three to five days, a tiny caterpillar hatches from each egg and spends its entire life on that milkweed plant just eating, excreting, and growing. In two weeks or so, when it reaches a couple of inches in length, it stops eating and builds a cocoon around itself. And inside this cocoon the most marvelous metamorphosis takes place: the lumbering, ugly, leaf-eating worm turns into a beautifully colored butterfly that flies off into the sky, only to descend every now and then upon a flower blossom to sip its nectar.

Of course in this world nothing lives forever; so after a few weeks the beautiful butterflies mate, the females produce eggs that they attach to the underside of milkweed leaves, and then they die. Except that in North America, in the fall, the butterflies start a two-thousand-mile migration trip to the South, either to coastal southern California or to the mountains of Central Mexico. Although there do exist recorded occasions of individual butterflies completing the entire trip, it usually takes two to three generations to finish it; with stops at milkweed patches along the way where new generations are produced to continue the journey. The generation that finally reaches its destination hibernates there for seven months before starting its return migration to the north.

And this (finally!) explains the title of the book. I believe that the current physical world represents the caterpillar stage of our life. Our souls, when they become physically unbound upon our death, correspond to the butterfly stage that we will enter. An era of freedom and.... Just as the caterpillar is completely incapable of understanding the life of the butterfly, just as the two-dimensional beings of *Flatland* (a wonderful little book written in 1884 by Edwin A. Abbott) could not comprehend the existence of three-dimensional beings, so we too cannot even imagine our future life.

Some readers may extrapolate from the butterfly analogy the existence of a closed universe where souls are reincarnated and remain forever in this world, but I disagree. If nothing else, the growth in human population during the last century invalidates the reincarnation concept, for there did not exist sufficient past souls to recycle. Besides, in chapter 7 we encountered a far more plausible explanation for the apparent reincarnation experiences.

But if this is all I wanted to say, you will ask, why did I take up so much of your time with all these other matters that I discussed in this book? Let me ask you this question: would you have bothered to buy and read a three-paragraph-long book?

BLISS

"You're not even listening, are you?!"

CHAPTER 12

IN CONCLUSION

Emigration to another country is a process of separation, one viewed differently by the various participants. The departing emigrant leaves behind his accustomed world and, looking forward with excitement and some trepidation, sets out for a new life of adventure and possibilities. The loved ones remain behind in their familiar environment to continue their usual old lives, but with a big gaping hole in their midst.

It is not only that somebody will have to take over the duties of the one who has left; that can usually be arranged. Irreplaceable, however, are the jokes that were said, the conversations that used to be exchanged, the moments of just sitting silently in each other's company. Eventually some letters will arrive from faraway with fascinating but very brief stories of a strange land and a perplexing way of life; but as time goes by these letters will probably become rarer and rarer until, eventually, they may stop altogether.

Death involves a similar type of separation. One leaves, heaven only knows for where, and the others remain behind, alone. They cannot even look forward to an occasional letter. Sometimes they attempt to talk to the departed, addressing the surrounding empty air or even going to the grave; but is there anyone to listen? This is the question that this book has tried to answer.

• • •

As a scientist there is one scene in the Old Testament that has always appealed to me. Prophet Elijah challenges the 450 priests of Baal to sacrifice a bull on a fire that their god will start. They pray all day but their God fails to respond and the woodpile remains unlit. Then Elijah orders some water thrown on his pile of wood, prays to God and miraculously the fire starts. The onlookers proclaim Elijah's God to be the true God, and in good Old Testament spirit the prophet orders that all of Baal's priests be immediately slain.

This is a miracle, however, that any self-respecting magician or even fledging chemistry student can repeat today. The hint lies in the statement that the fire started AFTER it was doused with water. Mix some powdered magnesium with wood, add water, and you have a fire. Firemen will tell you that water does not extinguish all fires; it starts some. I remember that in my freshman chemistry class I inadvertently set the contents of a garbage can on fire when I threw in the damp container a filter paper that had some sodium peroxide powder on it. Needless to say, I was never allowed to work alone in that lab again.

My point is not that Elijah had spread powdered magnesium on his firewood, but that there were many things in life that people did not know two millennia ago, and there are still many things that we don't know today. What, for instance, directs a dividing stem cell to become a hand rather than a foot or a heart? This book does not pretend to describe scientific facts verifiable by an attached list of laboratory experiments. Instead, it presents some theories of the more avant-garde scientists of our era and extrapolates some possible answers to a few of life's most important questions. Are they completely true? Probably not. Are they close to the truth? Who knows?

Is there a God? What is God? To some he is the divine being that is described in the pages of the Bible. To others he is love, the perfect prototype of the noblest emotion humans can feel. To others he is found in a beautiful sunrise or in the sight of a fluttering butterfly. To other it is nature. To still others, the self-styled atheists, he does not exist. With the exception of the first group, all of these just list a name, not a definition or a description. What does it mean to say that God is nature? What does it mean to say that one finds God in a beautiful sunset? Even the atheist must decide what kind of God he does not believe in. On the other hand, those who believe in the God Yahweh, the Father as described in the Bible, have a clear idea of what God is: he is a superman with superpowers too advanced for us to comprehend.

Another way to understand God is by the way he interacts with us. Is he a personal God? One who takes interest and occasionally answers our prayers and intervenes in our lives? Or is he an aloof power with a hands-off attitude? The first is called theism; the second, deism. The difference between the two is substantial. You pray to a theistic God but not to a deistic one. As for the atheists, in general they believe that only what they can prove in their laboratories exists. There is a word for that also, scientism. Their assertion prompts me to ask them whether they would suggest that we should stop looking for anything that is completely new. After all, their lab equipment is not designed to test for things that do not exist.

As I made very clear at the beginning, this is a personal book, describing my personal thoughts, ideas, experiences, and beliefs. Others may have different experiences and follow different reasoning to reach different conclusions. Maybe there is no such thing as objective Truth; perhaps we each have our own Truth. Perhaps, as this book has hinted, we may each affect our universe as much as it affects us.

To summarize my own thought process, I deduced the existence of a personal God because of some highly improbable occurrences in my life, which seemed to meet some of my apparent needs or feelings at the time they occurred. When I examined these events further, however, I came across various scientific explanations that do away with the need for an intervening God. According to these theories the universe is not what it seems to be but a mathematical illusion. And since, almost by definition, illusions are highly personal maybe the universe itself is personal. Maybe we make our own universe and we can thus affect it with our thoughts. Maybe matter is a pure illusion.

It appears that even some theologians agree with such conclusions. They argue that at the beginning there was only God, a non-material being, and thus the only available building material was himself. So he created the universe out of the only material he had available, his own essence. Tillich said that "God is the ground of all being," that everything else came forth from him. This is very similar to our subconscious, which every night creates the universe of our dreams. Is this world then just a figment of God's imagination? Such a concept would certainly explain everything, since everything is possible in a dream, but is it true? There is no way to tell from the inside where we are located. So somewhat in jest I suggested its scientific equivalent: that our world is a computer simulation, a cosmic video game. Substitute God for computer and both ideas are the same. But how does a dream end when there is no wake-up stage, death?

Being a scientist rather than a philosopher, I decided to opt for a real, material universe; keeping in mind, however, that all matter consists of energy and thus can be described in a mathematical formulation. I decided to go along with Ronald Tarter's hypothesis that God is an intelligent entity that resulted from the interaction of vibrating energy strings, the most basic structural elements of the universe but whose very existence has not been proven yet; not because I actually believe this to be true, but because it resolves the God problem. It gives my mind something real to wrap itself around, something it can comprehend.

To make sense in human terms, God must be something we can visualize, that not only serves a purpose but also embodies what we value most. The ancient Hebrews were surrounded by enemies and in constant danger of being annihilated. Their God promised them physical protection; he was a superman. A few centuries later, the philosopher-Christians could see the obvious inequities in life and its apparent hopelessness. Their God promised them a future life of justice, and encouraged them to start practicing it now; he was the morally perfect man, one to be emulated. Today's scientists prize the value of their mind and the understanding of the universe that it has brought them. Stephen Hawking, a powerful mind shackled to a wheelchair and unable to move a muscle, is, perhaps, the ultimate personification of a scientist. Scientists are unsure of God's existence, but if there is one, it must be a supermind.

If my God is true—and I don't insist that it is true—then this God is not the creator of the universe but part of its creation. But notice that even the Hebrew God did not create the universe from nothing: "In the beginning...the earth was a formless wasteland, and darkness covered the abyss" (Gen. 1:1-2). Yahweh just formed the Hebrew universe out of the available material.

In a similar manner Tarter's God helps form the scientist's universe out of the available material that, coinciding with modern theologians' ideas, is its own body. According to this hypothesis God arises from the interconnection between minute energy strings, and so does the universe. Perhaps these energy strings don't exist, but the concept remains the same: God is what everything is made out of, Tillich's "ground of all being." But whereas "ground of all being" is a general term that is fraught with ambiguity, the concept of the entire universe's energy interconnecting to form a humongous intellect provides a real image.

I then examined some paranormal events relating to dead people, most of which are described in published literature, but one that I personally experienced. I concluded that even if only a few of these events were indeed factual, then they would indicate that human memory and individuality survive one's physical death. And this can only be true if they exist outside the body in some kind of undiscovered field similar to the electromagnetic field that carries radio and TV programs. I defined an individual's soul as those memories that survive one's physical death. But be aware that the word "soul" is a very commonly used term and people assign to it many different definitions.

If our memories are indeed external and we continually access them and add to them while we are alive, then it is conceivable that we can also access memories that are not ours. Memories that belong to other people or even to this entity we name God. We call this last, inspiration, and I pointed out that many artists and scientists have acknowledged that ideas often appear into their minds in a fully completed form; one of them actually said that when inspiration struck him he felt as if he were looking directly into the mind of God.

Can we draw any lessons from all this analysis? What should we strive to accomplish during our few years here on this earth? Should we try to become the richest person in the world? The most powerful? The wisest? The one who will leave the grandest monuments or other edifices behind? None of these, I replied. I speculated that just as the purpose of the fetus is to prepare for the earthly life, our purpose on this earth is to prepare for the next one; to learn what will be of use to us in the hereafter, whatever that may be.

I then postulated that the most desirable attributes in that presumably spiritual world would be empathy and love. So these are the properties we should endeavor to cultivate while we are here. "Love your neighbor as yourself," is a good place to start. And where have you heard that expression? Yes, in a church, or synagogue, or some other similar place of spiritual enrichment. This explains why for decades now I have been attending weekly my local "House of God," despite all my reservations about the historical accuracy of his biography. What counts is not who this God is, but what he teaches. You don't select a college for its name but for its curriculum, the quality of its teachers, and the dedication of its students.

Let's bring our attention back to the submicroscopic energy strings that I postulated are the most basic structural elements of the universe. If these energy strings are indeed part of everything, then they must also be part of the memories that survive us, our souls. I guessed that in time these grow and connect with each other eventually merging with the whole entity itself, God. This, incidentally, was one of the basic beliefs of ancient Gnosticism: humans contain a divine spark that when released from the body returns to become reincorporated into its source, God. From the ancient to the super-modern and back to the ancient again, we have thus traced a full circle.

To conclude, just as I know that when the caterpillar reaches the end of its existence it turns into something more wonderful than it could have ever conceived, a beautiful butterfly free to soar at will...so I believe that when we reach the end of our mortal existence we will also be freed of our physical chains and turn into something completely new, wonderfully beyond our possible imagination. Our butterfly days are ahead! See you there, when our time comes!

(But if there is something you want to tell me that can't wait until then, do send me an e-mail at RegardingGod@aol.com).

WORKS CITED

Blum, Deborah. *Ghost Hunters: William James and the Search for Scientific Proof of Life after Death.* New York: The Penguin Press, 2006. The story of a small group of scientists who, led by the great psychologist William James, form the Society for Psychical Research to search for proof that human consciousness survives physical death. Interesting.

Bohm, David. *The Essential David Bohm*, Lee Nichol editor. New York: Routledge, 2003. An anthology of some of Bohm's writings explaining some of his theories and how they were developed. Very hard reading.

Church, F. Forester. *The Essential Tillich: An Anthology of the Writings of Paul Tilich.* Chicago: Chicago University Press, 1999. One of the first Christian philosophers to become widely known and quoted by clergy. The average person will find his writings are difficult to read and impossible to understand.

Combs, Allan and Mark Holland. *Synchronicity Through the Eyes of Science, Myth, and the Trick-*

ster. New York: Marlowe & Company, 1996. A fairly readable discussion of synchronicity, its similarity to Bohm's implicate and Sheldrake's morphic fields, and its relationship to myth and Hermes the trickster.

Haisch, Bernard. *The God Theory: Universes, Zero-Point Fields and What's Behind It All.* San Fransisco: Weiser Books, 2006. A scientist's effort to define and explain God. Readable and thought-provoking.

Hoeller, Stephan A. *The Gnostic Jung and the Seven Sermons to the Dead.* Wheaton, IL: Quest Books, 1982. Some information that is not widely disseminated regarding the origin of Jung's theories, and some of his side interests. Extraordinary.

Jung, C. G. *Synchronicity: An Acausal Connecting Principle.* Translated by R. F. C. Hull. Princeton, N.J.: Princeton University Press, 1973. Jung's brief original writing includes some of his astrological and numerological observations.

Moody, Raymond A., Jr. *Life after Life.* New York: HarperSanFransisco, 2001. The original work that described the near-death experience.

Rigas, Jim. *Christianity without Fairy Tales: When Science and Religion Merge.* Chapel Hill, N.C.: Professional Press, 2004. A scholarly yet very readable description of the Bible and its composition, the historical and scientific knowledge needed to understand it, and the rise of Christianity and its beliefs.

Ring, Kenneth, and Sharon Cooper. *Mindsight: Near Death and Out-of-Body Experiences in the Blind.* Kearney, Neb.: Moris Publishing, 1999. Do blind see during their near-death experiences? The authors say yes, after a fashion.

Sheldrake, Rupert. *A New Science of Life: The Hypothesis of Morphic Resonance.* Rochester, VT.: Park Street Press, 1995. A unique theory of creation and of the real world around us.

Schwartz, Gary A. *The Afterlife Experiments: Breakthrough Scientific Evidence of Life after Death.* New York: Atria Books, 2002. Scientifically controlled experiments with selected mediums are interpreted as events of contact with the spirits of dead people. Interesting, if true, but existence of telepathy can also explain the results.

Talbot, Michael. *The Holographic Universe.* New York: HarperCollins Publishers, 1991. A unique theory about how everything and everybody are interconnected. Not too difficult.

Tarter, Ronald Lewis. *The God Theory.* Baltimore: PublishAmerica Book Publishers, 2002. A very interesting monograph summarizing science and evolution from the Big Bang to the String Theory. It concludes by defining God as the intelligence that results from the interconnections between all the hypothetical energy strings in the universe, in direct analogy to the human intelligence that arises from the interconnections between the neurons in the human brain. Easy.

Wilson, Timothy D. *Strangers to Ourselves: Discovering the Adaptive Unconscious.* Cambridge, Mass.: The Belknap Press of Harvard University Press, 2002. Most of our learning during life takes place unconsciously, and although we use it during our decision process it remains consciously inaccessible. A small, but very interesting book.

INDEX